Anonymous

The Book of Order

Rules and forms of procedure of the Presbyterian Church of England together with

the Model Trust Deed

Anonymous

The Book of Order
Rules and forms of procedure of the Presbyterian Church of England together with the Model Trust Deed

ISBN/EAN: 9783337381240

Printed in Europe, USA, Canada, Australia, Japan

Cover: Foto ©Lupo / pixelio.de

More available books at **www.hansebooks.com**

THE

BOOK OF ORDER

OR

RULES AND FORMS OF PROCEDURE

OF THE

𝕻resbyterian Church of England

TOGETHER WITH THE

MODEL TRUST DEED

REVISED EDITION.

LONDON
PUBLISHING OFFICE OF THE
PRESBYTERIAN CHURCH OF ENGLAND
14, PATERNOSTER SQUARE

1894

PREFACE TO THE FIRST EDITION.

THE BOOK OF ORDER lays down and describes the form of Government in the PRESBYTERIAN CHURCH OF ENGLAND. The distinctive features of this Church are—1st, That its doctrines are Trinitarian and Evangelical; 2nd, That its Government is representative in character, and is in the hands of Teaching and Ruling Elders, duly elected by the members of the Church; and 3rd, That by its gradation of Courts, viz., the Session, the Presbytery, and the Synod, provision is made for the good government of the Church in things spiritual, the preservation of the rights of its members, and the maintenance of good discipline; whilst the administration of the Finances of the Church in its several congregations is entrusted to Deacons' Courts or Boards of Managers.

Presbyterian Government, in the language of the Formula, is held in the Church "to be founded on, and agreeable to, the Word of God," and is believed to have been substantially the mode of Government prevalent in the Apostolic Churches. The form of Government adopted by most of the Churches which at various dates separated from the Church of Rome was Presbyterian. The Waldensian Church was constituted on that form. The same was partially introduced in Switzerland in 1541. It made its way into France in 1555, and it has ever since been the form of Church Government of many of the Protestant Churches on the Continent of Europe as well as America. The first General Assembly of the Church of Scotland met in 1560. The first meeting of a Presbytery in Ireland took place at Carrickfergus in 1642. And in 1572 a Presbytery was formed at Wandsworth, Surrey, in England.

In 1646–1647 [1] the Church of England was constituted as a Presbyterian Church, and, at the passing of the Act of Uniformity in 1662,[2] the great majority of the ejected Ministers were Presbyterians. A large number of Presbyterian congregations continued to exist in England, notwithstanding altered and adverse circumstances; but they were unhappily torn by internal discords, and suffered from want of Presbyterial superintendence. Meanwhile the Church of Scotland, and the Secession and Relief Churches, which afterwards became the United Presbyterian Church, as well as the Reformed Presbyterian Church, planted several congregations here and there in England.

In 1836 two Presbyteries, comprising English congregations of the Church of Scotland, together with several of the old English Presbyterian congregations, were organised into a Synod. In 1839 two other Presbyteries joined the same, when it was decided to adopt the title of "The Synod of the Presbyterian Church in England in connection with the Church of Scotland." To these other Presbyteries subsequently adhered.[3] At the disruption of the Church of Scotland in 1843 that Synod asserted its independence of the Scottish Church, and in 1849 the words "in connection with the Church of Scotland" were removed from the title. The "Presbyterian Church in England" remained thus constituted from its first formation in 1836 till 1876, when, by the action of their respective Synods, an incorporative union was effected between that Church and the English congregations of the United Presbyterian Church,

---

[1] Ordinance for the present settling without further delay of the Presbyterian Government in the Church of England. 5 June, 1646. Ordinance for the speedy dividing and setling the several Counties of this Kingdom into distinct Classical Presbyteries and Congregational Elderships. January 29, 1647. (Scobell's Acts.)

[2] 13 and 14 Car. II., c. 4.

[3] See Digest.

the United Church taking the name of "The Presbyterian Church of England."

On the constitution of this Church, its Law and Historical Documents Committee having been instructed to consider the whole subject of the forms and procedure in Church Courts, that Committee entrusted the preparation of the Rules of Procedure to a Sub-Committee, consisting of the Rev. Dr. Edmond, the Rev. W. Ballantyne, and the Convener. The late Presbyterian Church in England had since 1869 been engaged in preparing the Rules and Forms of the Church, part of which had been adopted by its Synod, and the other portions were nearly complete when the Union took place, while the United Presbyterian Section had its Book of Rules; a good basis therefore was at hand and available for the construction of the new Rules of Procedure.

In view, however, of the importance of bringing such rules into entire harmony with the extended character of the United Church, the Sub-Committee deemed it proper to enter into a minute and careful examination of the theory and practice of the Presbyterian form of Church government, as acted upon in both sections of the United Church as well as in other Presbyterian Churches, and made several reports on the subject to the Synod. The different parts of their labours were by the Synod remitted to the Presbyteries, for their consideration, and their emendations and observations were considered with the utmost care, first by the Sub-Committee, and afterwards in conference with deputies from the various Presbyteries of the Church. Many years' labour have thus been expended on the work. Some of the ablest and most experienced members from all the Presbyteries have been engaged in it, and it is believed to embody generally the acknowledged principles of Presbyterian polity.

The "Book of Order" is not a Code of Laws, but a representation of the consuetudinary practice or common law of the Church. Nor are the word "Courts" and "Judicial

Committee" used in the Church intended to convey the same meaning or legal sanction as in the case of Ordinary Law Courts. In its form of Church Government, as well as in all other matters connected with the Constitution and Worship of the Presbyterian Church, the leading principle in view is, "Let all things be done decently and in order."

LEONE LEVI,
Convener.

PREFACE TO THE REVISED EDITION.

THE SYNOD of 1887 resolved upon the revision of the Book of Order which had been recommended by the Synod of 1882 and extensively used throughout the Church. The revision was entrusted to the Committee on Law and Historical Documents, which was strengthened for this purpose by the addition of members skilled in the laws and practice of the Church. The Committee did not enter upon the work till the year 1838 when they received suggestions on the subject from Presbyteries. The methods followed by the Committee in carrying on the work, the progress made in it, and the objects aimed at in relation to it, were regularly laid before the Synod from the beginning till the end of the Committee's labours.

The time spent upon it has not been more than its importance required. A sense of that importance actuated the members of the Committee in all the attention and care with which they did this work which they felt to be a sacred service for the good of the Church and the glory of God. The Committee, thankful for all aid in their protracted labours, commend this revised edition of the Book of Order to the blessing of God, and hope that in many ways it may prove helpful in the various departments of the life and work of the Presbyterian Church of England for a great while to come.

WILLIAM BALLANTYNE,
Convener.

CONTENTS.

	PAGE
PREFACE TO FIRST EDITION	v
PREFACE TO REVISED EDITION	viii
EXTRACT MINUTES OF SYNOD	xii

CHAPTER I.
THE CHURCH.

SECTION	I. Standards	1
	II. Membership	1
	III. Government	2
	IV. Relation to other Churches	2

CHAPTER II.
THE CONGREGATION.

SECTION	I. Constitution and Membership	5
	II. Formation of New Congregations	6
	III. Ministerial Support	6
	IV. Meetings	7
	V. Congregational Mission Stations	8

CHAPTER III.
THE SESSION.

SECTION	I. Constitution	9
	II. Election and Admission of Elders	9
	III. Meetings	11
	IV. Functions and Duties	12

CHAPTER IV.
THE DEACONS' COURT OR BOARD OF MANAGERS.

SECTION	I. Constitution	15
	SUB-SECTION A. The Deacons' Court	15
	B. The Board of Managers	16
	II. Meetings	16
	III. Functions and Duties	17

CHAPTER V.

THE DIACONATE.

		PAGE
Section	I. Constitution	19
	II. Meetings	20
	III. Functions and Duties	20

CHAPTER VI.

THE PRESBYTERY.

Section	I. Constitution	23
	II. Meetings	25
	A. Ordinary	25
	B. *In hunc effectum*	27
	C. *Pro re natâ*	27
	III. Functions and Duties	28
	IV. Theological Students and Probationers	29
	V. Vacancy in the Pastorate	31
	VI. Election and Call of a Minister	32
	VII. Ordination of Ministers	34
	VIII. Transference and Induction of Ministers	35
	IX. Admission of Ministers, Congregations, Probationers, and Students of Theology from Churches with which Mutual Eligibility has not been established	37

CHAPTER VII.

THE SYNOD.

Section	I. Constitution	39
	II. Meetings and Procedure	40
	III. Functions and Duties	42
	A. Legislative	42
	B. Administrative	43
	C. Judicial	44
	IV. Close of Synod	45

CHAPTER VIII.

COMMISSION OF SYNOD.

Appointment, Members, Meetings, Procedure 46

CHAPTER IX.

RULES OF PROCEDURE COMMON TO ALL THE COURTS.

Section	I. Overtures	47
	II. References	48
	III. Dissents	49
	IV. Complaints	50
	V. Appeals	50
	VI. Procedure in case of Complaint or Appeal	51
	VII. Petitions	53

CHAPTER X.

DISCIPLINE.

Section		Page
I.	Nature and Ends of Discipline	54
II.	Grounds for Discipline	54
III.	Subjects of Discipline	55
IV.	Raising of Charge of Offence	55
V.	Statement of Charge	56
VI.	Citation	56
VII.	Procedure in Summary Trials	58
VIII.	Procedure in Trial upon an Indictment	58
IX.	Rules of Evidence	61
X.	Church Censures	63
XI.	Removal of Censures	64
XII.	Courts Administering Discipline	65
	A. Sessions	66
	B. Presbyteries	67
	C. The Synod	68

APPENDIX.

A.	STANDING ORDERS OF SYNOD	71
B.	SUSTENTATION FUND ACT	76
C.	AGED AND INFIRM MINISTERS' FUND	80
D.	MINISTERS' WIDOWS' AND ORPHANS' FUND	81
E.	HOME MISSION	85
F.	EMPLOYMENT OF PROBATIONERS	94
G.	THE THEOLOGICAL COLLEGE	97
H.	FORMULAS	103
I.	CALLS	107
J.	EDICTS	109
K.	CERTIFICATES	112
L.	COMMISSIONS	114
M.	NOTICES	115
N.	DECLARATIONS	117
O.	AFFIRMATION	118
P.	MEMORIAL OR PETITION	118
Q.	MINUTES:—	
	A. Of Session	119
	B. Of Deacons' Court or Board of Managers	126
	C. Of Congregational Meetings	129
	D. Of Presbytery	130
R.	MODEL TRUST DEED	130

EXTRACT MINUTE OF SYNOD

Held at London, on the 27th April, 1882.

"*Inter alia:*—The Report of the Law and Historical Documents Committee was laid on the table by Dr. Leone Levi, *Convener.*

Resolved:—Receive the Book of Order, instruct the Law and Historical Documents Committee to complete and index the same, including with it the Model Trust Deed; and deeming it useful in maintaining uniformity in the procedure of the Church, adopt the same, and recommend its use in all the Courts of the Church, as well as in Congregations, and by Boards of Managers, with the understanding that all the rules are subject to the provisions contained in the Trust Deeds and to authorised constitutions, whether sanctioned by their respective Presbyteries or otherwise."

EXTRACT MINUTE OF SYNOD

Held at London, on the 27th April, 1886.

"*Inter alia:*—The Report of the Law and Historical Documents Committee was laid on the table by Dr. Leone Levi, *Convener.*

Resolved:—That the Synod agree to recognise the Book of Order as a correct statement of the consuetudinary practice of the Church, and recommend it to the Congregations and inferior Courts for their guidance."

EXTRACT MINUTE OF SYNOD

Held at London, on the 3rd May, 1894.

"*Inter alia:*—The Synod called for the Report of the Committee on Law and Historical Documents, which was given in by the Rev. W. Ballantyne, Convener, who addressed the House on the subject, and laid on the table a complete copy of the Revised Book of Order.

Resolved:—That the Report be received, that the thanks of the Synod be given to the Committee for their labours on the revision of the Book of Order, that they be directed to insert in it the regulations adopted by this Synod respecting the new Church Building Fund, also the new regulations on the Admission of Students to the College, and that they be authorised to issue it without delay for general use."

THE BOOK OF ORDER

OF THE

Presbyterian Church of England.

CHAPTER I.

THE CHURCH.

Section I.—Standards.

1. The Presbyterian Church of England holds that the Word of God, contained in the Scriptures of the Old and New Testaments, is the only Rule of Faith and Duty. *Standards*

2. The Westminster Confession of Faith and the Larger and Shorter Catechisms are the Subordinate Standards of this Church. In subscribing the said Standards, the Office-Bearers of the Church hold that, "while Civil Rulers are bound to render obedience to Christ in their own province, yet they ought not to attempt in any way to constrain men's religious belief, or invade the rights of conscience." The Formulas in use at Ordinations and Inductions connect the XXIV. "Articles of the Faith" adopted by the Synod of 1890, with the Westminster Standards, as more briefly expressing "the body of doctrine" these Standards set forth. They also refer to the "Appendix to the Articles of the Faith," as "expressing the general opinion and belief entertained in the Church on the matters to which it refers."

3. The Westminster Directory for Worship sets forth generally the order of public worship, of the preaching of the Word, and of the administration of the Sacraments, in this Church. *Worship.*

Section II.—Membership.

4. The Membership of the Church consists of all persons who are Members of its separate Congregations. *Membership.*

Each Member is entitled to the privileges, and is subject to the jurisdiction, of the Church.

Section III.—Government.

Courts.
5. The Government of the Church is vested in Courts, designated respectively, Sessions, Presbyteries, and Synod in regular gradation of authority, in the order named.

Moderator's Vote.
6. Each of these Courts is presided over by a Moderator, or President, who has not a deliberative vote, but, in case of equality on a division, has a casting vote.

Prayer.
7. Every Meeting of each Court is opened and closed with Prayer, and this must be recorded in the Official Minutes of each Meeting.

All Courts open.
8. All the Courts are ordinarily open to the Members of the Church, but it is competent for any of them to sit with closed doors, on any occasion, recording at the time in the Minutes the reason why the Court so resolves.

Absence of Members.
9. A Member of any Court unable to be present at a Meeting may send an apology for absence. Should his apology be accepted by the Court, he has a right to dissent from any decision come to in his absence.

Appeal to Civil Tribunal.
10. An appeal from a decision of any of its Courts to a Civil Tribunal is regarded by the Church as a grave offence.

Section IV.—Relation to Other Churches.

A.—The United Presbyterian Church.

Federal Relationship.
11. The Synod, in 1876, established with the Synod of the United Presbyterian Church a federal relationship which maintains and manifests the unity of the Churches by mutual interest and co-operation to as great an extent as is consistent with separate and independent jurisdiction.

How carried into effect.
12. This relationship is carried into effect as follows:—

(*a*) "Each Church recognises the status of the Ministers, Elders, Deacons, Probationers, and Members of the other, as if they were its own; and Congregations of the one Church are at liberty to obtain pulpit supply from the other."

(*b*) Corresponding Members, not exceeding six, are appointed by the Supreme Court of each Church to attend the meetings of the other, with right to deliberate, but not to vote.

B.—THE FREE CHURCH OF SCOTLAND.

13. The fraternal tie which long subsisted between the Presbyterian Church of England and the Free Church of Scotland was drawn closer when, in 1889, the Synod of the former Church and the General Assembly of the latter, entered into such a relationship as maintains and manifests their unity by mutual interest and co-operation to as great an extent as is consistent with separate and independent jurisdiction. *Federal Relationship*

14. This relationship is carried into effect as follows:— *How carried into effect.*

   (a) "Each Church recognises the status of the Office-Bearers and Members of the other as if they were its own; and the Ministers and Probationers of the one are eligible for Calls by any Congregation of the other, in the same way as if they were its own."

   (b) Corresponding Members, to the number of not more than six, are appointed by the Supreme Court of each Church to attend the meetings of the other, with right to deliberate, but not to vote.

   (c) The Supreme Courts of the two Churches concur in Regulations as to Attendance at the Theological Colleges of the Free Church and the Theological College of the Presbyterian Church of England.

[See *in Appendix—Regulations for Admission to the Theological College.*]

C.—FEDERAL COUNCIL OF THE THREE CHURCHES.

15. The federal relationship established by the Synod in 1876 with the Synod of the United Presbyterian Church was enlarged in 1889 by the entrance of the Free Church into federal relations with the Presbyterian Church of England and the United Presbyterian Church, and is carried into effect by a Federal Council consisting of twenty members appointed by the Supreme Court of each of these three Churches, which meets at fixed times (usually every third year), to deliberate on their common interests, and, without exercising legislative or judicial functions, to aid and advise in questions of difficulty and importance submitted to it by the Supreme Court of any one of the three Churches. *Federal Council.*

D.—THE PRESBYTERIAN CHURCH IN IRELAND.

16. The fraternal relations between the Presbyterian Church of England and the Presbyterian Church in Ireland are carried into effect as follows:— *Fraternal Relationship.*

How carried into effect.

(*a*) In one year, Deputations expressive of brotherly affection and interest are sent from the Supreme Courts of the two Churches to each other; and in the next, Letters to the same effect are sent, and so on alternately.

(*b*) The Ministers and Probationers of the one Church are eligible for Calls by any Congregation of the other, in the same way as if they were its own.

[See *in Appendix—Regulations for Admission to the Theological College.*]

E.—THE CALVINISTIC METHODIST CHURCH OF WALES.

Fraternal Relationship.

17. The fraternal relations between the Presbyterian Church of England and the Calvinistic Methodist Church of Wales are carried into effect by the appointment of corresponding Members to the Supreme Courts of both Churches, by the joint action of the Churches in special districts, and by the appointment of a Joint Committee of twelve members—six from each Church—selected every three years, to take steps to carry into practical effect certain resolutions on points of co-operation adopted by the Synods of both Churches in 1886.

F.—THE REFORMED CHURCHES HOLDING THE PRESBYTERIAN SYSTEM.

Presbyterian Alliance.

18. The Church is a member of "The Alliance of the Reformed Churches throughout the World holding the Presbyterian System," and is represented at its Meetings in General Council, from time to time (usually every fourth year), by delegates appointed by the Synod, "to confer upon matters of common interest, and to further the ends for which the Church has been constituted by her Divine Lord and only King."

CHAPTER II.

THE CONGREGATION.

SECTION I.—CONSTITUTION AND MEMBERSHIP.

19. A fully organised Congregation consists of the Office-Bearers and other Members of the Church in full Communion, together with their children. Persons not in full Communion, who are seat-holders, or who otherwise statedly support ordinances, and who ordinarily worship along with the Congregation, are usually called Adherents, and form part of the Congregation, but they have not the right of voting at the election of a Minister or Office-bearers, or on matters belonging exclusively to the Members in full Communion. *Members.*

20. A Congregation is under the spiritual charge of a Session, and its secular affairs are under the care of a Deacons' Court, Board of Managers, or Committee of Management. *Government.*

21. All baptised persons who make a profession of faith in Christ, and lead a life consistent therewith, may be admitted by the Session to Membership in full Communion. In the case of persons who have not been baptised, Baptism is administered previous to admission into full Communion. A Session admits to Membership in full Communion persons bringing Certificates of Church Membership in other Congregations. *Admission of Members.*

22. A Member is in full Communion with the Congregation so long as his[1] name remains on its roll of Communicants, cases of suspension under discipline excepted. *Continuance of Membership.*

23. Members in full Communion have the right of access to the Lord's Table, and are entitled to Baptism for their children, and to vote in the election of the Minister and other Office-Bearers of the Congregation. *Rights of Members.*

24. A Member in full Communion, when leaving a Congregation, is entitled to receive a Certificate of Membership. *Certificate of Membership.*

---

[1] In all cases where the Masculine Gender is used in this Section, or in any other part of this Book, the words are to be read as including the Feminine also.

THE BOOK OF ORDER.

Right of Petition.
25. A Member may present a Petition or Memorial to the Session regarding any matter which, in his judgment, may affect his spiritual interests, or those of others.

Access to Presbytery and Synod.
26. Members have access to the Presbytery and Synod by Petition or Memorial through the Session. Should the Session refuse to transmit the same, the Petitioners may appeal to the Presbytery.

SECTION II.—FORMATION OF NEW CONGREGATIONS.

Preaching Station.
27. Any number of persons in a locality wishing to be supplied with public religious ordinances may apply for that purpose to the Presbytery within whose bounds they reside; and if the Presbytery grant their application, it establishes in the locality a Preaching-Station of the Church, which it places under an existing Session, or a provisional Session, or a Committee appointed for the purpose.

28. A Preaching-Station may also be originated by the initiative of the Presbytery itself.

Raising of a Preaching-Station to a Congregation
29. A Preaching-Station may be raised by the Presbytery to the position of a fully organised Congregation; but in cases in which aid from Synodical funds is required towards the maintenance of ordinances, the authority of the Synod must be previously obtained.

Formation of new Congregation.
30. An application made to a Presbytery for the formation or recognition of a new Congregation is laid on the table, and a Committee is appointed to inquire into the following particulars:—1. The causes and circumstances that have led to the application; 2. The means of grace provided in the district; 3. The building proposed to be used by the Congregation for worship, and its distance from neighbouring Churches; 4. Whether any neighbouring Congregation has any objection to offer to the application; and 5. The probable means of supporting ordinances. The Committee having reported, the Presbytery decides according to the general interests of the Church.

SECTION III.—MINISTERIAL SUPPORT.

Support for Minister.
31. A Congregation, before applying to the Presbytery to take the necessary steps in a Call, decides what provision it is prepared to make for the support of the Minister. This is intimated to the Presbytery in the Schedule required by the Sustentation Fund Act, or by the Commissioners sent to the Presbytery. The Commissioners also give to the Presbytery such other information regarding the finances, prospects, and general condition of the Congregation, as the Presbytery may require.
[See *Sustentation Fund Act, Appendix.*]

32. Should a Congregation at any time thereafter be unable to pay the Stipend intimated to the Presbytery, it cannot of itself reduce the amount, but must inform the Presbytery of the circumstances, with a view to such other arrangement as may be found practicable or expedient. — Stipend.

33. If there be reason to believe that the Stipend or other pecuniary obligation of a Congregation is in arrears, although no communication has been made of the same, the Presbytery institutes inquiries, and takes such action in the case as the circumstances may require. — Action of Presbytery in such case.

Section IV.—Meetings.

34. An Annual Meeting of the Congregation is held to receive a Financial Report from the Deacons' Court or the Managers for the past year, to appoint Auditors, and also to transact such other business as may be regularly brought before it. At such Meeting the Session usually reports, for information, on the whole work of the Congregation for the year. — Annual Meeting.

35. No Meeting of the Congregation can be held except by the authority of the Session or of a superior Court. — Authority for Meeting.

36. The chair at a Congregational Meeting called for spiritual purposes is taken by the Moderator of Session. If the Meeting be called for secular purposes, the chair may be taken either by the Moderator of the Session, or by such other Member of the Church as may be chosen by the Meeting, prescriptive rights from usage or otherwise being reserved. — Chairman.

37. All Meetings of a Congregation should be convened by public intimation on the Lord's Day, a reasonable interval being allowed after the intimation. — Notice of Meetings.

38. All Members in full Communion have the right to vote for the Election of Trustees of the Church buildings and other Congregational property. — Voting for Trustees.

39. A Meeting for the Election of Trustees must be summoned by intimation from the pulpit on two successive Lord's Days. It may be presided over by the Minister, or by any other Member of the Congregation chosen for the purpose. The names of the persons elected as Trustees should be certified by the Chairman of the Meeting, at and in the presence of the Meeting. — Meeting for Election of Trustees.

40. Minutes of Congregational Meetings held for spiritual purposes are embodied in the Records of the Session, and those of Meetings for other purposes in the Records of the Deacons' Court or Board of Managers. — Minutes.

Section V.—Congregational Mission Stations.

Under care of Session.
41. A Congregational Mission Station is under the care of the Session of the Congregation with which it is connected.

Admission to Membership.
42. Admission to membership at a Congregational Mission Station is by the Session of the Congregation with which it is connected, in the same manner and under the same rules as in the case of an ordinary Congregation.

Roll of Members.
43. The names of the Members in full Communion at a Congregational Mission Station may, with the approval of the Presbytery, be placed on a Roll separate from that of the Roll of Members of the Congregation with which it is connected.

Rights of Members.
44. Members at a Congregational Mission Station, whose names are on a separate Roll, have all the rights and privileges of Members of the Church, as set out in paragraphs 22–26, but are not entitled to vote in any matters pertaining to the Congregation with which the Station is connected.

CHAPTER III.

THE SESSION.

Section I.—Constitution.

45. A Session consists of the Minister, or Ministers, and the Ruling Elders of a Congregation. The Minister presides as Moderator. *Members.*

46. If there be more Ministers than one, they preside alternately, unless otherwise agreed between them.

47. In the temporary absence of the Moderator, any Minister of the Church or any Member of the Court deputed by the Moderator, may preside. *Absence of Moderator.*

48. During a vacancy in the Ministerial office, or the absence of the Minister on leave obtained, the Presbytery appoints one of its Ministerial Members as temporary Moderator of the Session. *Case of Vacancy.*

49. If there are no Elders in a Congregation, or if the number is insufficient, the Presbytery appoints Elders from within its bounds to act as Members of Session until the deficiency is supplied. *Appointment of Elders by Presbytery.*

50. Of its own motion, or on application from a Session, the Presbytery may in special circumstances add to a Session members from any other Session, or Sessions, within its bounds; such appointment to continue so long as the Presbytery deems it to be expedient.

51. In any special case, the Presbytery, on application by a Session, or of its own motion, may appoint some of its members as Assessors to the Session, with the right to sit and vote with the Members thereof in the special case. *Appointment of Assessors.*

52. The Session appoints a Clerk, whose duty it is to keep a roll of its Members, take minutes of its proceedings, and take charge of Sessional papers, books, and documents. *Session Clerk.*

Section II.—Election and Admission of Elders.

53. The Session determines when to hold an Election of Elders, and fixes the number required. *Election of Elders.*

THE BOOK OF ORDER.

Electors.

54. The Elders are elected by the Members of the Congregation in full Communion.

Intimation and mode of Election.

55. An election of Elders having been determined upon by the Session, an intimation of its decision is made from the pulpit on two successive Lord's Days, and Members in full Communion are invited to choose from among themselves persons suitable for the office; Or, the Session may, if it see fit, propose certain persons for election by the Members. The Session thereafter, by an open vote at a Meeting convened for the purpose, by voting papers, or otherwise, ascertains the choice of the Members, and declares accordingly.

Who are eligible.

56. Only Members of the Congregation in full Communion are eligible to the Eldership.

Sustaining of Election.

57. An election to the Eldership having been made, the Session considers as to each person, whether, in all the circumstances of the case, the election shall be sustained, and his admission proceeded with. The election having been sustained, and no appeal against that decision having been taken, the Session notifies it to the person or persons elected, and takes steps to obtain his or their acceptance of the office.

Steps previous to Ordination.

58. The Session having received notice of acceptance of the office, appoints a time for the Ordination or Induction, and directs intimation thereof to be given to the Congregation from the pulpit on two successive Lord's Days.

59. Such intimation should contain a notice that if any Member have any objection to the life or doctrine of any of those elected, the objection must be stated to the Session at a Meeting, the time and place of which should be specified, and that if no objection be then and there stated, the Ordination or Induction will take place at the time appointed.

Objection to Ordination.

60. If any objection be stated, the person or persons objecting are called upon to substantiate the same.

If the Session find that the objection is frivolous, or unsupported by evidence, its duty is to proceed with the Ordination or Induction as appointed, unless an appeal be taken against its judgment.

If the objection appear to the judgment of the Session to be serious, and supported by *primâ facie* evidence, it declines to proceed with the Ordination or Induction of the person or persons objected to, until the matter has been duly investigated.

If the result of the investigation be to sustain the objection, the election becomes void.

61. The Ordination or Induction usually takes place on the Lord's Day, at one of the services of public worship. *Ordination and Admission.*

The Session having been constituted, the Moderator gives a narrative of the proceedings connected with the election.

He then puts to the persons elected the questions prescribed in the Formula.

[See *Formula, Appendix.*]

On receiving satisfactory answers, he, in the case of persons not previously ordained as Elders, ordains them by special prayer, accompanied, if it be thought desirable, by the laying on of hands, and thereafter declares them inducted into office in the Congregation. In the case of persons formerly ordained as Elders, he, after special prayer, declares them inducted into office in the Congregation.

The Moderator then declares those thus ordained or inducted to be Members of the Session, and gives them the right hand of fellowship, as do also the other Members of Session present.

The Moderator afterwards exhorts both the newly admitted Elders and the people.

The names of the new Members are thereafter added to the Roll of Session.

62. Elders hold office in a Congregation until they cease to be Members thereof in full Communion, or until the Session accepts their resignation, or declares them to be no longer Members of the Court because of absence from its Meetings for a period of not less than twelve months not satisfactorily explained, or until they be judicially deprived of their office. *Tenure of Office.*

Section III.—Meetings.

63. The Session holds stated Meetings for the transaction of ordinary business, intimation thereof having been previously given from the pulpit. *Ordinary Meetings.*

64. The Session may be convened, in case of urgency, by the authority of the Moderator, or by appointment of a superior Court, either by intimation from the pulpit, or by notice sent to the Members. *Special Meetings.*

65. The Moderator must convene the Session on the requisition of three of its Members.

66. No meeting of Session can be held at an hour when the Presbytery of the bounds is holding an Ordinary Meeting, or when the Synod is sitting, except by permission of these Courts.

12 THE BOOK OF ORDER.

Quorum. 67. The Moderator and two other Members of Session constitute a quorum.

Record of Proceedings. 68. The Session is held responsible by the Presbytery for the regular and faithful keeping of its Records.

Names of Members. 69. The names of the Members present at each meeting are inserted in the Record.

Reading of Minutes. 70. Before proceeding to other business, the Minutes of last Meeting are read, and, if approved as a true record of what was done, are signed by the Moderator and Clerk, provided the same has not been done at the close of that Meeting.

71. In approving or correcting the Minutes, the Session cannot alter what was done at the former Meeting.

Alteration in Minutes. 72. If alterations be made in the Minutes by the deletion or the insertion of any word or words, they are noted on the margin, and are attested by the initials of the Moderator and Clerk.

Extracts from Minutes. 73. Extracts from Minutes of Session are given, on request, to Parties in any Case, and are certified by the Clerk.

SECTION IV.—FUNCTIONS AND DUTIES.

Duty of Session. 74. It is the duty of the Session to rule over the Congregation in spiritual matters, and to promote the religious interests of all connected with it.

Public Worship. 75. The Session fixes the times of public worship, authorises and regulates the administration of the Sacraments, and appoints special times for humiliation, or thanksgiving, or prayer.

Service of Praise. 76. The Session exercises superintendence over the Service of Praise in the Congregation, and, with the concurrence of the Deacons' Court, or Board of Managers, as to financial arrangements, makes the necessary appointments in connection with that Service.

Responsibility to Presbytery. 77. The Session is responsible to the Presbytery for the manner in which public worship is conducted, and the Sacraments administered.

78. The Minister is responsible for the discharge of his duties, not to the Session, but to the Presbytery of which he is a Member.

Admission of Members. 79. The Session admits to the Membership of the Congregation, either on the acceptance of a Certificate of Church Membership from another Congregation, or on being satisfied with the qualifications of the applicant as to knowledge and character.

80. The Session keeps a Roll of the Members of the Congregation in full Communion, which should be annually revised and attested by it, and should be submitted to the Presbytery annually, for attestation by it also, and at other times, when called for. *Roll of Communicants.*

81. The Session also keeps a Roll of all baptised Members of the Congregation not yet in full Communion. *Roll of baptised Members.*

82. The Session fixes a term, not less than one year, and not more than two years, beyond which the name of a Member shall not be continued on the Roll of Communicants, if, without satisfactory reason given, he has not taken his place at the Lord's Table, or has not otherwise availed himself of his religious privileges in connection with the Congregation. *Continuance on Roll.*

83. The Session must grant a Certificate to any Member not under discipline applying to be disjoined from the Congregation. *Certificate of Disjunction.*

84. Before any step is taken in the election of a Minister, the Session has the Roll of Communicants made up to the time of application to the Presbytery to grant opportunity for giving a Call, and attested by the Moderator and Clerk, and a copy thereof is laid on the table of the Presbytery. *Making up the Roll.*

85. When the appointment of special or ordinary collections is not exclusively under the superintendence of the Deacons' Court or Board of Managers, such collections are appointed by the Session, after consultation with the Court or Board, if thought desirable. *Collections.*

86. It is the duty of the Elders to visit the sick, arouse the careless, instruct the young, guide and encourage inquirers, edify and comfort believers, and, generally, promote the welfare of the Congregation. *Duty of Elders.*

87. The Session receives and judges of petitions presented by Members on matters connected with the doctrine, discipline, or government of the Congregation, or of the Church as a whole. *Petitions.*

88. The Session determines when there shall be an election of Deacons in the Congregation, and fixes the number required. *Election of Deacons.*

89. The Session receives and decides upon the resignation of both Elders and Deacons. *Resignation of Elders and Deacons.*

90. The Session is responsible for the institution and management of Sunday Schools in connection with the congregation. *Sunday Schools.*

Representative in Presbytery.

91. The Session elects a representative Elder to the Presbytery. Such representative Elder is ordinarily one of its own number; but, in exceptional circumstances, a Member of another Session within the Presbytery may be elected. If the representative Elder elected die or resign within the period for which he has been elected, a new election is made for the remainder of the period.

Representative in Synod.

92. The Session elects a representative Elder to the Synod from its own number, or, in exceptional circumstances, from any other Session of the Church.

CHAPTER IV.

THE DEACONS' COURT,

OR

THE BOARD OF MANAGERS.

Section I.—Constitution.

Sub-Section A.—The Deacons' Court.

93. The Deacons' Court consists of the Minister or Ministers, Elders, and Deacons, three making a quorum. — Membership.

94. Deacons are elected, and ordained, or inducted in the same manner, and under the same rules, as Elders, the Formula for Deacons being used at Ordination or Induction. They also hold their office under the same conditions as Elders. — Election. Ordination.

[See *Formula in Appendix*.]

95. The Court appoints a Clerk and one or more Treasurers. — Clerk.

96. The Clerk keeps minutes of the proceedings, and takes charge of the books, papers, and documents belonging to the Court, except such as are entrusted to the Treasurers. — Treasurers.

97. The Treasurers receive and account for all the moneys under the care of the Court. Their accounts are submitted quarterly, or at other stated intervals, to the Court, and are audited at least once a year.

98. The Minister of the Congregation presides over the Deacons' Court; but, in his absence, any Member of the Court may be chosen to preside. — Chairman.

99. If there be more Ministers than one, they preside alternately, unless otherwise agreed between them.

100. The presiding member, called the Chairman, has not a deliberative vote, but, in case of equality on a division, has a casting vote. — Chairman's Vote.

Sub-Section B.—The Board of Managers.

Election. 101. The Managers, who must be Members in full Communion, are elected by their fellow-members. The election takes place at the Annual Meeting of the Congregation, or at some other duly appointed time, notice of which is given at least three days previously from the pulpit.

Rules of Election. 102. If rules as to the election are prescribed by the Constitution or the Trust Deeds of a Congregation, these rules must be observed.

Retiring Managers. 103. In most cases, one-third of the elected Managers retire each year. The retiring Managers are eligible for re-election.

Managers *ex officiis*, and by Election. 104. In some Congregations the Board of Managers consists of the Minister and Elders *ex officiis*, together with a certain number of Managers, who are elected by the members of the Congregation, as set out in paragraph 101.

Chairman. 105. In these cases, the Board so constituted is commonly designated the Committee of Management, of which the Minister is the Chairman. The Clerk and the Treasurer or Treasurers are appointed by the Committee itself.

106. In the absence of the Minister, any Manager, duly chosen by a majority of those present, may preside.

Chairman's Vote. 107. The Chairman has not a deliberative vote, but, in case of equality on a division, has a casting vote.

Election of official Members. 108. In those cases in which the Board of Managers does not include the Minister and Elders *ex officiis*, the Congregation either elects the Chairman, Treasurer, and Clerk of the Managers, or empowers the Board to appoint them from their own number.

Auditors. 109. At the meeting for the election of Managers, the Congregation elects two of its own members as auditors of accounts, who, previous to next annual meeting, are to examine the Treasurer's books and vouchers for the year, and report thereon to said next annual meeting.

Section II.—Meetings.

Ordinary Meetings. 110. The Deacons' Court, or the Board of Managers, in ordinary circumstances, meets monthly, and is convened either by intimation from the pulpit or by written personal notice to the members, sent or given by the Clerk in sufficient time before the meeting. Three members form a quorum.

111. A Special Meeting is summoned by the Chairman, either on his own authority, or on the requisition of three Members of the Court or Board. — *Special Meetings.*

112. In case of necessity, in the absence of the Chairman, the Clerk calls a meeting on the requisition of three Members of the Court or Board.

113. The rules as to the minutes and the proceedings of meetings of the Court or Board are the same as for Sessions. — *Minutes.*

Section III.—Functions and Duties.

114. The Court or Board administers the temporal affairs of the Congregation. — *Duties.*

115. It has charge of all the property belonging to the Congregation, takes care that it is kept in good condition and repair, and receives the funds needful for the purpose. — *Property.*

116. It has charge of all the funds belonging to the Congregation, or held by Trustees for its use, lets the seats, collects the seat-rents, receives the subscriptions to the Sustentation Fund, and other contributions; and it applies these funds to the purposes for which they have been contributed. — *Funds.*

In aid-receiving Congregations it sends to the Ministerial Support Committee the whole balance of the ordinary income of the Congregation remaining after meeting the Congregational expenses allowed by the Committee; furnishes the Committee, through the Presbytery, with an annual statement of its accounts signed by two duly appointed auditors; and, in the case of a vacancy in the Pastorate, prepares the Schedule required before asking for opportunity to call a Minister.

117. It also receives and applies contributions for the poor of the Congregation, except in cases in which provision is made for the care and relief of the poor by the Session. — *The Poor.*

118. It has no power to contract debt on the security of the property without the explicit authority of the Congregation and the approval of the Presbytery. — *Debt.*

119. It appoints and dismisses the Church-officer, door-keepers, and other subordinate officials, and fixes their salaries. — *Officials and Salaries.*

120. In concurrence with the Session, it makes or cancels the necessary appointments in connection with the Service of Praise in the Congregation.

121. It makes arrangements for fulfilling the financial — *Collections.*

appointments of the Synod in regard to the Schemes of the Church. It also appoints special collections or subscriptions to be made for objects which it judges to be deserving of the support of the Congregation.

Report. 122. It lays a statement of its accounts, duly audited, and a report of its proceedings, before the annual meeting of the Congregation.

Discipline. 123. It has no power of discipline, but it is entitled to certified extracts from the minutes of Session in so far as the resignation, removal, suspension, or deposition of any office-bearer affects its own membership. Any change of which it thus receives evidence is recorded in its minutes.

Use of Buildings. 124. It is not entitled to give the use of any ecclesiastical buildings belonging to the Congregation for any purpose whatever without the consent of the Minister, nor to withhold the use of these buildings for meetings of a strictly religious, ecclesiastical, or charitable nature, which have the sanction of the Minister, or Moderator of Session for the time being.

These buildings are not to be used for any meeting which is not strictly of a religious, ecclesiastical, or charitable nature without the express consent of both the Minister and the Court, or Board.

Spiritualia. 125. It has no authority over the spiritual order of the House of God, or over the conduct of Public Worship in any of its parts.

Appeal. 126. An appeal may be taken from it to the Presbytery, and to the Synod, upon any matter within its own province, such appeal being transmitted through the Session.

Right of the Session. 127. The constitutional right of the Session to watch over all the interests of the Congregation, and, if necessary, to intervene by calling a meeting of the Congregation, or in any other competent manner, is expressly reserved.

CHAPTER V.

THE DIACONATE.

Prefatory Note.

The Synod, in 1888, instructed the Committee on Law and Historical Documents, which was then engaged on the revision of the Book of Order, "to consider and report upon the steps to be taken with a view to greater uniformity in the constitution of Congregations in its bearings upon Deacons' Courts and Boards of Managers." The result of the Committee's action, as so instructed, was laid before the Synod on successive occasions in a Chapter combining into one the systems prevalent in the Church for the conduct of the secular affairs of congregations by Deacons' Courts, or Boards of Managers, sometimes designated Committees of Management. That Chapter, having been transmitted by the Synod to the Presbyteries of the Church for their consideration, was finally revised by the Committee in the light of suggestions received from the Presbyteries, and was laid before the Synod of 1893 in the form in which it is here given. The following resolution respecting it was adopted by that Synod :—"That the Chapter on the Diaconate be printed in the Book of Order in different type from the rest of the Book, and be preceded by a recommendation of Synod that its provisions should be adopted wherever possible, in order to secure greater uniformity in the constitution of Congregations."

I.—Constitution.

128. The Diaconate consists of the members of Session and the Deacons, sitting together. — Members.

Election.	129. Deacons are elected by the members in full communion from among themselves, for a limited time, or for life, as may be determined by the Session.
	130. Deacons for a limited time are elected at the Annual Meeting, or at a special meeting of the congregation, or otherwise, as the Session may determine, and, after they have been elected, are set apart to their duties with prayer, in presence of the congregation. The Formula for Deacons may be used.
Ordination. Induction.	131. Deacons for life are elected, and ordained or inducted in the same manner and under the same rules as Elders, the Formula for Deacons being used at ordination or induction. They hold their office under the same conditions as Elders.
Treasurers. Clerk.	132. The Diaconate appoints one or more Treasurers, and a Clerk. The Treasurers receive and account for all the moneys under the care of the Diaconate. The accounts are submitted at stated intervals, and audited once a year before being presented to the annual meeting of the congregation. The Clerk keeps minutes of the proceedings, and takes charge of the books, papers, and documents, except those entrusted to the Treasurer or Treasurers.

II.—Meetings.

Ordinary and Special.	133. The Diaconate, in ordinary circumstances, meets monthly, and all its meetings, ordinary and special, are convened and conducted under the same rules as those of the Session.
President.	134. The Minister of the congregation presides over the Diaconate; but in his absence any member may be chosen to preside.
	135. If there be more Ministers than one, they preside alternately, unless otherwise agreed between them.

III.—Functions and Duties.

Administration.	136. The Diaconate administers the temporal affairs of the Congregation, collecting the contributions of the Congregation, and disposing of them for the purposes for which they have been collected, administering the general revenues of the Congregation, taking charge of the property, keeping the

buildings in good condition and repair, and raising the funds necessary for this purpose, and attending to the poor.

137. The Diaconate organizes and oversees the Association for obtaining contributions to the Sustentation Fund, and observes the other requirements of the Sustentation Fund Act. In aid-receiving congregations the Diaconate sends to the Ministerial Support Committee the whole balance of the ordinary income of the Congregation remaining after meeting the Congregational expenses allowed by the Committee; furnishes the Committee, through the Presbytery, with an annual statement of its accounts signed by two duly appointed auditors; and, in the case of a vacancy, prepares the Schedule required before Moderation in a Call is asked for. *Sustentation Fund.*

138. The Diaconate arranges for the fulfilment of the financial appointments of the Synod in regard to the Schemes of the Church. It appoints special collections or subscriptions for objects which it considers deserving of the support of the Congregation. *Synod Schemes.*

139. Before Moderation in a Call is asked for by a Congregation, the Diaconate, with the concurrence of the Congregation at a meeting duly called, determines what provision shall be made for the support of the Minister. It appoints one or more of its members as commissioners to the Presbytery to give information as to the finances of the Congregation. *Support of Minister.*

140. The Diaconate proposes any subsequent increase, or reduction, of the Minister's stipend which it considers advisable, and submits the same for approval to a meeting of the Congregation; but no reduction of the amount reported to the Presbytery before the settlement of the Minister can be made without the consent of the Presbytery. In the case of a proposal to reduce the stipend of the Minister, the Diaconate reports to the Presbytery, and appoints one or more of its members as commissioners to state the circumstances to that Court. *Stipend.*

141. If the Presbytery has reason to believe that the Diaconate has fallen into arrears in respect of stipend or other pecuniary obligations, although no communication has been made of the same, the Presbytery institutes inquiries, and takes action as the case may require. *Arrears.*

Appointment of Officials.

142. The Diaconate concurs with the Session in appointing and dismissing the leader of the Public Praise, and itself appoints and dismisses other officials.

Finance.

143. The Diaconate submits statements of finance for the year, duly audited, to the Annual Meeting of the Congregation, and reports on its management of the other temporal affairs of the Congregation.

Debt.

144. The Diaconate cannot contract debt on the security of the property without the approval of the Congregation and the Presbytery.

Discipline.

145. The Diaconate has no power of discipline, but it is entitled, for its information, to certified extracts from the minutes of Session in so far as the resignation, removal, suspension, or deposition of any office-bearer affects its membership. Any change of which the Diaconate thus receives evidence is recorded in its minutes.

Use of Buildings.

146. The Diaconate is not entitled to give the use of any ecclesiastical buildings belonging to the Congregation for any purpose whatever without the consent of the Minister, nor to withhold the use of these buildings for meetings of a strictly religious, ecclesiastical, or charitable nature, which have the sanction of the Minister or Moderator of Session for the time being.

Appeal.

147. An appeal may be taken from a decision of the Diaconate to the Presbytery and Synod upon any matter within its province. Such appeal must be transmitted through the Session.

Trust Deeds.

148. The Diaconate, in all its proceedings, must have due regard to the provisions of Trust Deeds and authorized Constitutions.

CHAPTER VI.

THE PRESBYTERY.

Section I.—Constitution.

149. The Presbytery is the Court of the Church immediately above the Session.

150. A Presbytery consists of:—   Members.

    (a) The Ministers of all the Congregations within the bounds assigned to it by the Synod.
    (b) Professors of Theology whose sphere of labour is within the bounds.
    (c) Such ordained Ministers as the Synod may determine.
    (d) Representative Elders chosen, one by the Session of each Congregation within the bounds.

151. A Presbytery may associate with itself *pro tempore*, with the right to speak, but not to vote, any member of another Presbytery, either of this Church, or of any sister Church, who may be present.   Associates.

152. Ministers and Elders from other Presbyteries may be added by the Synod as Assessors to a Presbytery for particular purposes.   Assessors.

153. Before an Elder takes his seat in the Presbytery, he presents a duly certified Commission from the Session which he represents. If he is a Member of another Session, he presents also a Certificate from that Session that he is an acting Member thereof.   Elder's Commission.

154. An Elder's Commission may be made out for twelve months, or six months, at the discretion of the Session which appoints him.   Period of Commission.

155. An Elder's Commission, in due form, is received and sustained at any Meeting of Presbytery.   Receipt of Commission.

156. On his Commission being sustained, his name is added to the Roll of the Presbytery, and, if present, he takes his seat in the Presbytery.   Seat in Presbytery.

Election of a Successor.	157. In the event of the death or retirement of a Representative Elder, or of his suspension or removal from office, a successor is elected by the Session which he represented, within a month, or as soon as possible thereafter.
Tenure of Seat in the Presbytery.	158. An Elder duly enrolled, continues a Member of the Presbytery during the term of his Commission, usually for twelve months, in some cases for six months, at the discretion of the Session, unless he resign or be judicially deprived of his office.
Termination of Commissions.	159. Elders' Commissions all terminate at the close of the Annual Meeting of the Synod, and new Commissions are called for at the first Ordinary Meeting of Presbytery thereafter.
Official Members.	160. The Officials of the Presbytery are the Moderator, the Clerk or Clerks, and, where required, the Treasurer or Treasurers.
Moderator.	161. The Moderator is chosen from the Ministers who are Members of the Court.
Moderator pro tempore.	162. In the absence of the Moderator, or in the case of his leaving the chair, his predecessor in office, or, failing him, another Minister presides, who, in signing any document officially, must add to his signature the words *pro tempore*.
Moderator's Functions.	163. The Moderator opens and closes each meeting of the Presbytery with prayer. He sees that order is preserved in the conduct of business, and protects each Member of the Presbytery in the exercise of his rights. He rules on points of form and order. He takes precedence of the Members, but is in all matters subject to the Presbytery. He is the official organ of the Presbytery in announcing decisions, administering rebukes and admonitions, instructing parties at the bar, and calling upon Members to state their views, to give their votes, or to discharge any duties which have been assigned to them. He does not take part in any debate upon the merits of the question in debate; but by permission of the Presbytery, he may leave the chair in order to do so, or to make a motion, the chair being for the time occupied by another Minister.
Question of Order.	164. The Moderator protects speakers from undue interruption or annoyance; and on any Member raising a question of order while another is speaking, the speaker resumes his seat till that question is disposed of by the Moderator.
At Ordination.	165. At the Ordination or Induction of a Minister or Professor of Theology, at the Ordination of a Medical

Missionary to the Eldership, and at the Licensing of Probationers, the acting Moderator puts the questions of the Formula, and offers up prayer as appointed. He also delivers the appointed addresses, unless the Presbytery has otherwise arranged.

166. If the Moderator is a party in a case, he must vacate the chair while the case is under adjudication. *Leaving the Chair.*

167. The Clerk and the Treasurer are chosen by the Presbytery, and are usually Members thereof, in which case they retain all their rights. *Clerk. Treasurer.*

168. The Clerk keeps the roll of the Members, minutes the proceedings of the Presbytery, takes charge of its records and papers, and under its authority gives extracts from its minutes to those entitled to them. In his absence, another is appointed to act *pro tempore*. *Clerk.*

169. The Treasurer has charge of the funds and accounts of the Presbytery, and reports on the same at appointed times. *Treasurer.*

Section II.—Meetings.

170. Three Members, two of whom must be Ministers, form a quorum. *Quorum.*

171. A Presbytery holds its stated meetings at certain set times and places, but may also meet at such other time and place as it may arrange and appoint. No Presbytery can meet beyond its own bounds, or within them, while the Synod is assembled, except by the permission of the Synod. *Meetings.*

172. Should a quorum not be present on the appointed day for an ordinary Meeting, or should a day not be appointed for the next ordinary Meeting, the Presbytery lapses, and cannot again meet for business until convened by special summons of the Moderator to all the Members, either on his own authority, or at the request of two or more of its Members, or by the authority of the Synod. In the first or second case, the Presbytery must report the circumstances to the Synod at its next Meeting. *Failure and Revival of Meeting.*

A.—Ordinary.

173. An ordinary or stated Meeting is one held (*a*) by adjournment from a previous ordinary or stated Meeting, as often as the Presbytery shall see cause; (*b*) by special appointment of Synod; (*c*) in consequence of the revival of the Presbytery in a constitutional manner, as set forth in Paragraph 172. *Ordinary Meeting.*

Such Meeting is for the transaction of whatsoever business may arise.

Minutes.	174. After an ordinary Meeting has been constituted with prayer, the Clerk reads the Minutes of the preceding Meeting or Meetings, except that if the Minutes of these Meetings are printed, and in the hands of the Members, they are held as read; and when they are pronounced to be correct, they are sustained, and are then signed by the Moderator in the Chair and by the Clerk.
	175. The Minutes, however, may be framed as the business proceeds, and, if read and sustained, are then signed at the close of the Meeting.
Alteration in Minutes.	176. If alterations be made in the Minutes by the deletion or the insertion of any word or words, they are noted on the margin, and are attested by the initials of the Moderator and Clerk.
Order of Business.	177. It is customary, and ordinarily expedient, for the Presbytery to take up, first, personal matters, then business arising from the Minutes in its order, and afterwards, other matters as the Presbytery may arrange.
Notice of Motion.	178. In case of the introduction of matters of importance, by motion or otherwise, notice thereof must be given at an ordinary Meeting previous to that at which they are to be considered. If such matters are not brought forward at the Meeting stated in the notice, they cannot be taken up without the renewal of the notice, except by special permission.
Motion. Amendment.	179. The proper mode of submitting any proposal for the adoption of the Presbytery is by Motion, and the proper mode of opposing it is by a counter Motion or Amendment. A Motion, when seconded, can neither be withdrawn nor altered without the consent of the Presbytery.
	180. If a Motion or Amendment is not seconded, it is not before the Presbytery, and is not recorded.
Right of Speaking on Motion.	181. No Member is entitled to speak on the merits of a Motion more than once, with the exception of the mover, who, in case of an Amendment, has a right to reply. A Member, however, may be permitted to make an explanation subject to the ruling of the Moderator.
Question put.	182. When there are two Motions before the Court, the question put to the vote is, First, or Second Motion? or, Motion, or Amendment?
Order of Voting.	183. When there are more than two Motions before the Court, the vote is taken on the several Motions successively, in the order in which they were proposed; and unless it appears that one of the Motions has a clear majority of all the votes, that which has the lowest

number is dropped, and a fresh vote is taken upon those that remain, till one of them is finally carried. The Motion carried is afterwards put as a substantive Motion, the question being, Aye, or No? or, For, or Against?

184. The Presbytery, annually, or at such times as it judges convenient, calls for the Communion Rolls of the Congregations within its bounds, or for Extract Minutes of the Sessions, certifying that such Rolls have been duly revised, and stating the number of names therein. *Communion Rolls.*

185. It also calls annually, or at such times as it judges expedient, for the Records of Sessions. *Session Records.*

B.—*In hunc effectum.*

186. A Meeting *in hunc effectum* is one appointed at an ordinary Meeting of the Presbytery for some special business which must be stated at the time of appointment and recorded in the Minutes. *In hunc effectum.*

187. At a Meeting *in hunc effectum* that part of the Minutes of the ordinary Meeting specifying its appointment and the business for which it is held is read. *Minutes.*

188. No other business can be transacted at a Meeting *in hunc effectum* than that for which it has been specially appointed. *The only Business.*

C.—*Pro re natâ.*

189. A *pro re natâ* Meeting is one summoned by the Moderator between ordinary Meetings, for cases of emergency requiring immediate attention, sufficient time being allowed to the Members to attend. *Pro re natâ.*

190. The Moderator may summon a Meeting *pro re natâ* either on his own responsibility, or on a requisition from two or more of the Members whose requisition states their reason for desiring the Meeting to be summoned. *How called.*

191. The Moderator, however, may decline on such requisition to call the Meeting; but, in that case, he must state the facts and his reason for not complying with the requisition at the next ordinary Meeting of the Presbytery, and abide its decision. *Moderator's declinature to call it.*

192. The business for which a *pro re natâ* Meeting is called must be stated in the summons sent to the Members. *Statement of Business.*

Section III.—Functions and Duties.

193. The Presbytery :—

(a) Takes care that the Word of God is preached, the Ordinances of Divine Worship duly observed, the Sacraments regularly administered, and the various duties of the Ministry discharged in the Congregations within its bounds.

(b) Takes cognisance of all matters relating to the condition of the Congregations within its bounds.

(c) Receives and decides questions, and determines references, complaints, appeals, and petitions from Sessions, and also petitions from members of the Church transmitted through Sessions.

(d) Takes the oversight of the Missions, and the Week-day and Sunday Schools belonging to its Congregations.

(e) Originates and recognises Preaching Stations and new Congregations.

(f) Sanctions the erection of new Churches and other buildings, and approves of the sites and plans for the same.

(g) Sees that provision is made for the supply of vacant pulpits; ordains Probationers to the office of the Ministry; inducts Ministers into their pastoral charges, and looses them therefrom.

(h) Sets Missionaries apart for work at home and abroad.

(i) Examines Students of Divinity and licenses them as Preachers and Probationers.

(j) In case of discipline by Indictment, the Presbytery, after consultation, if judged necessary, with the Synodical Committee of Advice on Judicial Procedure, or with the Legal Adviser of the Church, appoints a Committee to frame the Indictment, and on the Indictment being approved and served, to act as prosecutors in the case.

(k) Discusses Overtures and other matters sent down by the Synod, and sends up Petitions and Overtures to the Synod on any subject calling for notice or reform.

(l) And, generally, the Presbytery has power over its own Members, Sessions, Congregations, Students, Licentiates, and Schools, and over all matters which the Synod may from time to time commit to its charge and supervision.

194. The sanction both of the Presbytery and the Synod is required for any sale or transference of Churches, Manses, or other Buildings, or Lands, which by title-deeds have become the property of the Church; but money may be borrowed by mortgage or otherwise on said property, with the consent of the Presbytery alone. Sale of Property. Borrowing of Money.

195. A Presbytery has no legislative powers and functions. Not legislative.

196. It is the duty of the Presbytery as a Court to execute the laws and observe the injunctions issued by the Synod, and to see that all subject to its jurisdiction, in their several places and relations, do the like. Laws of the Church.

SECTION IV.—THEOLOGICAL STUDENTS AND PROBATIONERS.

197. Presbyteries hold inter-sessional Examinations of Theological Students preparing for the Ministry of this Church on prescribed portions of the Hebrew and Greek Scriptures, on Bible Knowledge, the Standards of the Church, and Personal Religion. Examinations.

198. When the Student has completed the prescribed curriculum, and has passed the Exit Examination by the College Board of Examination, he presents the necessary certificates to the Presbytery within whose bounds he resides, and is then taken on trials for licence as a Preacher of the Gospel and a Probationer for the office of the Ministry. These certificates are:— Trials for Licence.

    (1) From the Professors, that he has fulfilled the appointed curriculum of study and satisfactorily performed all the prescribed exercises.

    (2) From the College Board of Examination, that he has passed the Exit Examination.

    (3) From the Session of the Congregation of which he is a member, that he has maintained a character becoming his position and views as a candidate for the Holy Ministry.

199. The Presbytery on being satisfied as to the piety of the Candidate and his motives for seeking to enter the Ministry, then prescribes to him the following discourses:— Discourses.

    (1) An Exegetical Analysis of some passage from the Hebrew Scriptures.

    (2) An Exegetical Analysis of some passage from the Greek Scriptures.

    (3) A Lecture or Expository Discourse on a passage of Scripture.

    (4) A Popular Sermon.[1]

---

[1] In ordinary practice Presbyteries usually call for the first,

200. The Presbytery appoints some of its Members to receive, examine, and report upon these discourses, and calls upon the Candidate to read such parts thereof as may be deemed expedient. He also preaches parts of the sermon before the Presbytery, and reads a portion of the English Bible.

Candidate transferred. 201. If the Candidate at any stage of his trials for licence removes beyond the bounds, the Presbytery, when satisfied with the cause of the removal, transfers him to the Presbytery within whose bounds he has gone to reside, certifying the subjects of trials that have been prescribed to him, and the parts that have been performed, whether with approbation or otherwise. The Presbytery to which he has been transferred then proceeds with those parts of his trials for licence which have not been previously passed with approbation.

Granting of Licence. 202. The Presbytery, on being satisfied with the trials of the Candidate, proceeds to grant him licence; and, in doing so, the following order is observed :—

> The Moderator puts to the Candidate the prescribed questions of the Formula. The answers being satisfactory, the Presbytery unites in prayer, and thereafter the Moderator addresses the Candidate in words to the following effect:—
>> In the name of the Lord Jesus Christ, the only Head of the Church, and by warrant and appointment of this Presbytery, I do hereby licence you to preach the glorious Gospel of the Grace of God, and declare you to be a Probationer for the Ministry of the Presbyterian Church of England. "Give diligence to present thyself approved unto God, a workman that needeth not to be ashamed, handling aright the word of truth."[1] "The Lord bless thee, and keep thee: the Lord make His face to shine upon thee, and be gracious unto thee: the Lord lift up His countenance upon thee, and give thee peace."[2]

Right hand of fellowship. 203. The Moderator having exhorted him to faithfulness and prayer, the Members of Presbytery give him the right hand of fellowship in the Lord.

---

second, and third of these discourses as delivered in the Theological College.

[1] 2 Tim. ii. 15 (R.V.).   [2] Num. vi. 24-26.

204. A Probationer is entitled to receive from the Clerk an attested extract Certificate of his licence. — *Certificate.*

[See *Rules for Employment of Probationers in Appendix*].

205. A Probationer or a Theological Student of any Presbyterian Church not yet within the range of mutual eligibility, seeking admission into this Church, must apply to a Presbytery, which examines his testimonials, and, if it sees fit, transmits the application with a report thereon to the Synod. — *Probationer or Student of another Church.*

Section V.—Vacancy in the Pastorate.

206. A vacancy in the pastoral charge of a Congregation arises from the death, resignation, translation, suspension *sine die*, or deposition of the Minister. — *How it arises.*

207. When a vacancy arises in the pastoral charge of a Congregation, the Presbytery appoints a Moderator of the Session *ad interim*, and orders that declaration of the vacancy be made to the Congregation, on the ensuing or next convenient Lord's Day, by one of its Members or by the officiating Minister and, at the same time, that the Congregation be called upon to take steps for the filling up of the vacancy, with all convenient speed, in accordance with the rules of the Church. — *Appointment of Moderator. Declaration of Vacancy.*

Vacancy by Death.

208. When a Minister in sole charge is removed by death, the Elders hold a Meeting, at which the senior Elder present presides, for the purpose of recording the Minister's death in the Minutes of the Session. — *Meeting of Elders.*

209. They direct that intimation of his death be made forthwith to the Moderator and the Clerk of the Presbytery, and they provide for the supply of the pulpit till next Meeting of the Presbytery. — *Notice to the Presbytery.*

Vacancy by Resignation.

210. A Minister who wishes to resign his Charge must tender his resignation to the Presbytery of which he is a member. — *Resignation of Minister.*

211. Permission to resign cannot be granted to a Minister against whom a judicial process has been commenced or a *fama* is known to exist. — *Permission to Resign.*

212. When a Minister applies for leave to resign, the Presbytery may order the application to lie on the table, appoint a Committee to confer with him regarding the reasons for the application, and cite the Session and Congregation — *Steps taken in case of Resignation.*

Reasons for Resignation.
to appear for their interests at a time and place appointed. If, however, the Session and Congregation have been duly informed of the Minister's purpose, and appear for their interests either by duly appointed representatives, or by the presentation of extract minutes of their concurrence, when the application is made, the Presbytery may dispose of the case at once.

213. If the reason be a change of opinion relative to the doctrine or polity of the Church, disqualifying him to continue in its Ministry, his resignation is at once accepted by the Presbytery, and he is declared to be no longer a Minister of this Church.

214. If the resignation be accepted for other reasons, the pastoral tie is dissolved, and the Pastorate is declared vacant; but he still remains a Minister of the Church. His name, however, is removed from the Roll of the Presbytery, unless the Synod shall otherwise direct.

SECTION VI.—ELECTION AND CALL OF A MINISTER.

Pulpit Supply.
215. When the Pastorate of a Congregation is vacant, it is the duty of the Session to provide supply for the pulpit, with a view to the choice of a Minister.

216. The Congregation, at a meeting duly called, may appoint a Committee of its Members to co-operate with the Session in that business.

Eligibility to a Call.
217. No one can be called to the Pastorate who is not a Probationer or a Minister of this Church, or of a Church whose Probationers and Ministers are eligible; namely, the Free Church of Scotland, the United Presbyterian Church, and the Presbyterian Church in Ireland.

Meeting for Election.
218. When the Session has reason to believe that there is a general desire in the Congregation to proceed to the election of a Minister, it duly summons a meeting of the Congregation to be held not earlier than after an interval of three entire days. The summons must state the object of the meeting.

Request to Presbytery.
219. Having ascertained that the Congregation is ready to proceed to the election of a Minister, the Session intimates this to the Presbytery at its next Ordinary Meeting, and requests that the usual steps may be taken for the calling of a Minister. If this meeting of Presbytery is not to be held within a calendar month, the Session may request the Moderator of Presbytery to summon a meeting *pro re natâ*.

Sustentation Fund.
220. The Presbytery, before taking steps for the settlement of a Minister, must see that the requirements of the

Sustentation Fund Act are observed. In the case of self-sustaining and aid-giving Congregations, the Presbytery also inquires as to the Stipend to be paid to the Minister.

[*See Sustentation Fund Act in Appendix.*]

221. The Presbytery, on granting the request from a Session for opportunity to a Congregation to elect a Minister, fixes a time for the election, appoints one of its Ministers to preside at the election, and directs that due notice thereof be given to the Congregation from the pulpit. *Appointment by Presbytery.*

222. The Congregation being assembled, and public worship having been conducted, the presiding Minister states the special object of the meeting and the order of procedure, and reads the Form of Call to a Minister. *Procedure at giving of a Call.*

223. Any Member in full Communion may then propose any eligible Probationer or Minister for election, and the motion being seconded, also by a Member in full Communion, put to the meeting, and carried, the person thus proposed is declared elected.

224. If two or more such Motions are made, the presiding Minister puts them to the vote in the manner prescribed in paragraph 183.

225. When the result of the vote, by show of hands or otherwise, is doubtful or challenged, the Roll of Members is called, and the votes are marked.

226. The person having the majority of votes is then declared elected, and his name is inserted in the Call.

227. The Office-bearers and Members are then invited to sign the Call; and, in the case of a division, the minority are urged to unite with the majority in signing the Call. *Signing a Call.*

228. Adherents who concur with the Members in giving the Call sign a separate declaration to that effect in a Form of Concurrence read at the meeting. *Adherents concurring in a Call.*

229. The presiding Minister attests the number of names adhibited to the Call and to the Form of Concurrence in his presence. *Attestation of signatures.*

230. The Call, including the Form of Concurrence, may be left for a specified time with the Session for additional signatures, which must be duly attested. *Call left with Session.*

231. The Minister appointed to preside at the giving of a Call reports to the Presbytery at its next ordinary meeting and lays the Call upon the table. *Call laid before Presbytery.*

D

232. In some cases the Call is brought up to the Presbytery by Commissioners from the Session and the Congregation.

Sustaining a Call.

233. The Presbytery, then, in view of all the circumstances, considers the question of sustaining the Call laid before it.

234. If the question of sustaining the Call be not decided at the meeting of Presbytery at which the Call is presented, a day not later than a fortnight thereafter must be fixed for its further consideration, and public intimation thereof must be made from the pulpit to the Congregation giving the Call.

Call to a Probationer or Minister without charge.

235. When a Call in favour of a Probationer or a Minister without charge is sustained by a Presbytery, the Clerk is directed to give him notice thereof, and to request intimation of his decision relative to the Call not later than a month thereafter. A longer period may be granted by the Presbytery in special circumstances.

[*For procedure in a Call to a Minister having a pastoral charge, see Section VIII.*]

Meeting of Presbytery at giving a Call.

236. In case of urgency, the Presbytery, instead of appointing one of its number to preside at the Election and Call of a Minister, may itself meet with a Congregation for that purpose, the method of procedure in both cases being the same. In that case, the Presbytery may at once, if it see fit, sustain the Call, and take further steps towards the settlement of a Minister.

Right of Appeal.

237. Parties in the case of a Call have the right of appeal to the Synod.

SECTION VII.—ORDINATION OF MINISTERS.

Trials for Ordination.

238. When a Probationer to whom a Call has been addressed intimates his acceptance of it, the Presbytery prescribes to him one or more subjects of sermon with a view to Ordination.

239. The Presbytery, having approved the sermon or sermons prescribed, appoints a day for his Ordination.

Appointment of Ordination.

240. The Presbytery appoints two or more Ministers to preach and preside at the Ordination and to address the newly-ordained Minister and the Congregation, and directs that the usual notice of Ordination be read to the Congregation from the pulpit, not less than three clear days being allowed between the reading of the notice and the day fixed for the Ordination.

241. The Minister appointed to preside at the Ordination is Moderator of the Presbytery on that occasion. *Moderator at Ordination.*

242. On the day of Ordination the Presbytery meets half an hour before the hour appointed for public worship to ascertain that the aforesaid notice has been duly read, and to call for objections, if any, to the character or the teaching of the Probationer whose Ordination has been appointed. *Presbytery Meeting for Ordination.*

243. If no objections are offered, the Presbytery proceeds to the Ordination.

244. After public worship and the preaching of the Word, the Moderator puts to the Probationer the questions of the Formula appointed to be put before Ordination. *Procedure at Ordination.*

[*See Formula in Appendix.*]

245. Satisfactory answers having been received, he is then ordained to the office of the Holy Ministry by prayer and the laying on of the hands of the Presbytery.

246. The Moderator then, in name and by authority of the Presbytery, declares him duly ordained to the office of the Holy Ministry, and also duly admitted and inducted into the pastoral charge of the Congregation, and entitled to all the rights and privileges belonging thereto.

247. In token thereof, the Moderator and the other Members of the Presbytery give to him the right hand of fellowship.

248. Addresses to the Minister and the Congregation are then delivered by the Moderator, and, at the close of the Service, the name of the Minister is added to the Roll of the Presbytery.

249. If any objection be made to the character or the teaching of the Probationer whose Ordination has been appointed, such objection, in order to be admissible, must be given in writing, and be supported on the spot by sufficient proof. If the objection is found to be trivial, or is not supported by sufficient evidence, the Presbytery sets it aside and proceeds to the Ordination. If the objection is not summarily set aside, the Ordination is postponed until the case is considered and decided according to the Rules of the Church. *Objection to Ordination.*

SECTION VIII.—TRANSFERENCE AND INDUCTION OF MINISTERS.

250. When the Call of a Congregation has been addressed to a Minister in a Charge in another Presbytery of this Church, and sustained, the Clerk of Presbytery *Call to Minister in a Charge.*

transmits it to the Clerk of the Presbytery of which the Minister is a member, together with extract minutes of relative proceedings, and a statement of reasons for his removal to the Congregation giving him the Call.

Commissioners. 251. One or more Commissioners may be appointed to appear before that Presbytery in support of the Call.

Procedure of Presbytery relative to said Call. 252. If the ordinary meeting of that Presbytery takes place within a calendar month after the Clerk thereof has received official notice that the Call has been given and sustained, the Presbytery takes up the Call at that meeting. The Clerk cites the Session and Congregation of the Minister to whom the Call has been given to appear for their interests at that Meeting.

253. If the ordinary meeting does not take place within one calendar month after the Clerk has received official notice that the Call has been given and sustained, a *pro re natâ* meeting is summoned by the Moderator for consideration of the Call, and to that meeting the Clerk cites the Session and Congregation whose Minister has been called.

254. The Presbytery being met, the Call and relative documents are read, and, if desirable, the Commissioners are heard. The Minister receiving the Call is asked to state his views. The Presbytery then, after prayer, considers and decides the case, and its decision is intimated to the parties by the Moderator. In some Presbyteries, prayer is offered before the Commissioners are heard.

Acceptance of said Call and its consequences. 255. If the Presbytery decide to put the Call into the Minister's hands, and he accepts it, the Presbytery dissolves the pastoral tie between him and his Congregation from that date, or from a date then fixed, and directs him to await the orders, relative to his Induction, of the Presbytery to which the Congregation whose Call he has accepted belongs.

256. The Presbytery gives him the right of ministering to his Congregation till and including the Lord's Day next following the date fixed for the dissolution of the pastoral tie,

257. The Presbytery instructs the Clerk to forward extract minutes of its proceedings relative to the Call to the Clerk of the Presbytery of which the Minister is to become a member.

Appointment of Induction. 258. On reception of these minutes, that Presbytery fixes the date of his Induction, appoints the Minister or Ministers who are to conduct the Service, and directs the usual notice to be given to the Congregation.

259. The Minister appointed to preside at the Induction is Moderator of the Presbytery *pro tempore*.

260. The order of Service at an Induction is the same as at an Ordination, with the exception of the laying on of the hands of the Presbytery. — *Service at Induction.*

261. In the case of an appeal being taken to the Synod against a decision of the Presbytery in the matter of a Call by any of the parties, or in the case of a dissent and complaint to the Synod being entered by a member of Presbytery against its decision in the same matter, proceedings are stopped until the appeal or the dissent and complaint is disposed of by the Synod. — *Appeal or Complaint.*

262. In the case of the Call of a Minister from one Congregation to another within the same Presbytery, the proceedings are the same as set forth in the previous parts of this Section, so far as applicable. — *Call to a Minister in his own Presbytery.*

263. In the case of the Call to a Minister of a Church which is on terms of mutual eligibility with this Church, the procedure is as stated in Section VI. of this Chapter. Procedure in support of such Call before the Courts of the Church to which the Minister called belongs is according to the Rules of that Church. — *Call to a Minister of another Church.*

SECTION IX.—ADMISSION OF MINISTERS, CONGREGATIONS, PROBATIONERS, AND STUDENTS OF THEOLOGY FROM CHURCHES WITH WHICH MUTUAL ELIGIBILITY HAS NOT BEEN ESTABLISHED.

264. When application for admission is made by a Minister of any such Church, the Presbytery appoints a Committee to confer with him, with instructions to inquire into and report upon :— — *Procedure on Application by a Minister.*

(1) His character, status, and service.
(2) The reasons which have led him to make the application.
(3) His education for the ministry.
(4) His Ordination.

265. If the Presbytery be satisfied, and approve the application, it reports the whole case to next Synod, and asks authority to admit the applicant according to the rules of the Church. — *Report to Synod.*

266. If the Synod grant authority to admit the applicant, the Presbytery requires him to answer the questions of the Formula for Ordination or Induction, and, after prayer and an address by the Moderator, admits him into fellowship, and declares him a Minister of this Church. — *Act of Admission.*

Application by a Congregation	267. If the applicant's Congregation also apply for admission, the Presbytery appoints the same or another Committee to inquire into all the circumstances of the Congregation, with instructions to report; and the Presbytery being satisfied, submits the case to the Synod, and asks authority to receive the Congregation as a Congregation of this Church.
Admission of Minister and Congregation.	268. Authority to receive both Minister and Congregation having been obtained, the Presbytery appoints a meeting with the Minister and Congregation on a convenient day, of which public intimation must be made from the pulpit to the Congregation, and, the Minister having answered the questions of the prescribed Formula, the Presbytery admits the Minister and Congregation, and inserts their names on the Roll of the Presbytery.
Congregation without a Minister.	269. When a Congregation without a Pastor desires admission, the Presbytery takes the course stated in paragraph 267, and, on the reception of the Congregation, appoints a temporary Session.
Probationers. Students.	270. In the case of Probationers or Students of Theology applying for admission, the Presbytery follows the same order as in the case of Ministers, so far as applicable, and, if satisfied, reports to the Synod. If authority be granted by the Synod, the Presbytery receives them as Probationers or Students of this Church, the former being required to give satisfactory answers to the questions of the Formula for Probationers.

CHAPTER VII.

THE SYNOD.

Section I.— Constitution.

271. The Synod is the supreme Court of the Church, and consists of the Ministers and Professors of Theology whose names are on the Rolls of the Presbyteries of the Church; of the ordained Missionaries of the Church; of Elders acting as Medical Missionaries or as Missionary Evangelists; of the Representative Ruling Elders, one appointed by each Session; and of such other Members as the Synod shall from time to time determine. {Members of Synod.}

272. Every Representative Ruling Elder produces a commission appointing him to represent a Session in the Synod, and in case of his not being a member of the Session which appoints him, he produces also a certificate from the Session of which he is a member that he is a *bonâ fide* Acting Elder. {Elder's Commission.}

273. The officials of Synod are the Moderator, who presides at its meetings, preserves order, takes votes, announces decisions, administers censures, and opens and closes each Sederunt with prayer; and the Clerk or Clerks, whose duty it is to keep the Roll of its Members, record its proceedings, preserve its papers, books, and documents, and give attested Extracts of its Minutes when ordered by the Court. {Official Members.}

274. The Synod elects as Moderator an ordained Minister of the Church.* {Moderator.}

275. The Synod appoints its Clerk or Clerks from time to time, as may be necessary. {Clerk.}

276. The Treasurership of the Synod Fund and of the general funds of the Church is vested in a Committee {Treasurership Committee.}

---

* By a resolution of Synod in 1880 the Moderators who have passed the Chair, together with Representatives appointed by the Presbyteries, are constituted a Board of Nomination, and, at the second stated meeting of the Standing Committees after the Synod, they select the name of the Minister who shall be proposed for the Moderatorship at next meeting of Synod.

appointed for that purpose, called the Treasurership Committee; and its Convener or Chairman for the time being is authorised to receive all Legacies, Bequests, and other moneys falling to the Church or any of its schemes, and to give full discharge for the same.

Section II.—Meetings and Procedure.

Annual Meeting. 277. The Synod meets annually at such time and place as have been appointed at the previous meeting.

Special Meeting. 278. The Synod may appoint a special meeting when it sees cause.

Meeting pro re natâ. 279. The Moderator has power, either on his own responsibility, or on the requisition of not fewer than fifteen members belonging to at least three Presbyteries, to summon a *pro re natâ* meeting in case of emergency.

Quorum. 280. Fifteen members, comprising both Ministers and Elders, provided that they belong to at least three Presbyteries, form a quorum.

Opening of Meeting. 281. The members having assembled at the time and place appointed, the Moderator of the previous Synod conducts public worship and preaches a sermon; and thereafter he constitutes the Synod with prayer in the name of the Lord Jesus Christ, the King and Head of the Church.

Roll of Members. 282. The Synod then makes up the Roll of members by placing thereon the names of all Ministers and Elders duly certified.

Election of Moderator. 283. The Synod next elects the new Moderator, who, on his appointment, is introduced by the retiring Moderator, and, having taken the chair, delivers an address.

Standing Orders. 284. The Standing Orders of the previous Synod are then read, or held as read, and, on being adopted, they regulate the conduct of business.

[*See Appendix.*]

Ministerial Changes. 285. The Clerk then submits a report of the changes that have taken place in the Roll of the Ministers of the Church since last meeting of Synod.

Committees. 286. Committees are then appointed as follows:—

1. On Elders' Commissions and on Records.
2. On Bills and Business.
3. On Selection.

287. Members of the Committee on Bills and Business are appointed, some by the previous Synod, and some by

Presbyteries as their Representatives. The Committee on Selection is formed by the appointment of the Conveners of the Standing Committees of Synod, and of Members nominated by the Presbyteries as their Representatives.

288. Each of these Committees has a Convener appointed by the Synod, and a Clerk, either appointed by the Synod or by the Committee itself.

289. No Committee may meet while the Synod is sitting without leave from the Synod. *Meetings.*

290. Regular Minutes of all Committees are kept by their respective Clerks, and the Minutes of a Committee may constitute its report to the Synod. *Minutes.*

291. All documents, such as Appeals, Complaints, References, Petitions, Overtures, etc., intended to be submitted to the Synod must be transmitted to the Clerk of Synod at least ten days before the meeting of Synod to be by him laid before the Committee on Bills and Business. *Documents for the Synod.*

292. The duties of the Committee on Elders' Commissions and on Records are:— *Duties of Committee No. 1.*

1. To examine such Elders' Commissions as the Clerk of Synod shall have reported to them to be defective or irregular.

2. To examine the Records of the Synod, of the Presbyteries, and of the Standing Committees of the Synod.

293. The duties of the Committee on Bills and Business are:—

1. To see that all the documents laid before them have been duly transmitted, are in due form, and are such as are proper to be brought before the Synod. Should the Committee refuse to transmit any document to the Synod it must intimate to the party or parties interested the ground of refusal. The Committee, however, may give liberty to amend a document, or otherwise to remove objection to its transmission. The Committee's resolutions for or against transmission may be brought under review of the Synod by appeal or complaint. *Duties of Committee No. 2.*

2. To recommend what shall be the order of business for each Session of Synod, taking care, in arranging the order, that the Reports of the Standing Committees shall, in accordance with the Standing Orders of the Synod, have such a place given them as may ensure due consideration.

Duties of Committee No. 3.

294. The duties of the Committee of Selection are:—

    1. To nominate, by direction of the Synod, such Committees as the Synod may see fit, from time to time, to appoint in the course of its business.

    2. To nominate the members of the Standing and the Special Committees of Synod for the ensuing year.

Synod in Committee.

295. The Synod, for the greater freedom of discussion, may resolve itself into a Committee of the whole House, in which case a separate minute is taken of the proceedings of the Committee. When the Synod resumes, the resolution or resolutions passed by the Committee are reported to the Synod, and are adopted by it without further discussion.

Call to Order.

296. Any member of the Synod has a right to call to order, and immediately on his doing so the member who is addressing the Synod should resume his seat until the question of order is determined. The member calling to order is then allowed to state briefly the ground on which the call to order has been made, but no other member is allowed to speak, unless with the permission or at the request of the Moderator, with whom the decision of the point of order entirely rests. Any member calling to order unnecessarily is liable to the censure of the Synod.

Rights of Speakers.

297. With the exception of the mover of a motion, who, in case of debate, has the right of reply, no member of Synod is permitted to speak more than once on the same question, unless to correct a mis-statement of fact, or to explain something which has been misunderstood.

Minutes.

298. The minutes of each day's proceedings are read, or held as read, and approved only at the morning sitting of the following day, with the exception of the minutes of the last day of the Synod, which are read and sustained before the close thereof.

Section III.—Functions and Duties.

A.—Legislative.

Jurisdiction.

299. The Synod, as the Supreme Court, exercises rule over all its Presbyteries, Sessions, and Congregations, and its decisions are final, and binding on the whole Church.

Matters taken up.

300. The Synod receives, considers, and takes action upon Reports, Appeals, Complaints, References, Petitions, Overtures, and other matters:—

    1. From Members of the Church, duly transmitted through Sessions and Presbyteries.

2. From Sessions, duly transmitted through Presbyteries.
3. From Presbyteries.
4. From Committees of Synod.
5. From individual Members of Synod.

301. Every proposal, by Overture or otherwise, which contemplates a material change in the constitution of the Church, or in its laws respecting doctrine, discipline, government or worship, must, if not dismissed by the Synod, be sent down to Presbyteries, for their consideration and report, before it can be passed into a standing law. *Proposals for new Legislation.*

302. Before giving judgment on a proposal sent down to Presbyteries for their consideration and opinion, the Synod calls for the returns from Presbyteries on the subject. *Returns from Presbyteries.*

303. If a majority of the Presbyteries disapprove the Overture, it is passed from. If a majority of the Presbyteries approve, the Synod proceeds to consider the question whether the Overture shall be adopted or not. If adopted by the Synod the Overture becomes a standing law. *Decision.*

304. The Synod, as it sees cause, sends proposals affecting the welfare of the Church, whether submitted by Overture or otherwise, to Sessions as well as Presbyteries, for consideration, and calls for Returns from these bodies before giving a decision on the proposals submitted. *Proposals sent to Sessions and Presbyteries.*

B.—*Administrative.*

305. The Synod takes the oversight of Presbyteries; erects new Presbyteries as circumstances may require; examines the records of Presbyteries, attests them, or remits them for correction, as may be judged necessary; judges of complaints and appeals against the decisions of Presbyteries; advises, exhorts, and censures Presbyteries and Parties, when necessary; disposes of Overtures, considers matters of common concern to the Church, whether respecting doctrine, worship, discipline, or government; issues addresses to Congregations; appoints special seasons of prayer and thanksgiving; declares testimonies in favour of truth and against error; maintains correspondence with other Churches; makes regulations respecting the College, appoints its Professors, Lecturers, and Examiners, and superintends its work; devises and regulates means for the adequate support of the Ministry; promotes and directs the Missionary operations of the Church at home and abroad; takes the oversight of the agencies of the Church for the religious instruction of the young; makes rules for the conduct of its own *General Administration.*

proceedings and those of the inferior judicatories of the Church; and, generally, attends to all matters relating to the interests and the work of the Church as a whole, or any part thereof.

Preaching Stations.

306. The Synod receives and decides on applications from Presbyteries for the raising of Preaching Stations to the Status of Sanctioned Charges in cases in which grants from any of the public funds of the Church are required towards the maintenance of ordinances.

Applications.

307. The Synod receives and decides on applications for admission into the Church from Ministers, Probationers, Theological Students, and Congregations of other Churches, such applications having been considered and transmitted by Presbyteries.

Committees for Administration.

308. The Synod appoints Committees to administer the various departments of the work of the Church from year to year:—
 (a) Standing Committees having charge of the permanent Schemes of the Church and their funds.
 (b) Special Committees having charge of matters specially assigned to them.

Collections.

309. The Synod appoints Collections to be made for the permanent Schemes of the Church, and for any other object it may judge important.

Decisions carried into effect.

310. According to the nature of each case, the carrying out of the decisions of the Synod is entrusted to the Synod's Committees, or to Presbyteries, or to Sessions, or to Commissions specially appointed.

C.—*Judicial.*

Procedure on References, etc.

311. As a Court of Review the Synod takes up and considers References, Appeals, Complaints, and Petitions, its procedure respecting them being similar to that of Presbyteries.

312. No question which belongs to the jurisdiction of an Inferior Court can be considered by the Synod unless it has been duly brought up by Reference, Appeal, Complaint, or Petition.

Judicial Committee.

313. The Synod appoints from year to year a Committee of Advice on Judicial Procedure, called the Judicial Committee, to examine papers and to consider the facts and circumstances which may be laid before it by Presbyteries in cases of difficult Judicial Trial, and to give such counsel as may be deemed expedient.

Judicial Trials.

314. All matters pertaining to Judicial Trials, the competency and effect of evidence in such cases, and the

procedure of Presbyteries therein, may come up before the Synod by Reference, Appeal, Complaint, or Petition.

315. In dealing with questions of evidence, the Synod must form its judgment from the full record of the evidence transmitted by the Clerk of the Inferior Court, with due attention to the pleading of the Parties at its own bar. *Evidence.*

316. If any irregularity or defect is found in the record of the proceedings of the Inferior Court in a Judicial Trial, the Synod may correct it. *Correction of irregularity or defect.*

Section IV.—Close of Synod.

317. The business of the Synod having come to an end, the Moderator delivers an address, declares the Synod dissolved, and appoints the next Synod to be held at the time and place previously agreed upon, and the proceedings are closed with praise and prayer. *Proceedings at close of Synod.*

CHAPTER VIII.

COMMISSION OF SYNOD.

Appointment.
318. A Commission of Synod is appointed by the Synod, as it sees cause, for the discharge of functions specifically assigned to it; one-third of the members appointed to form a quorum.

Members.
319. The members of a Commission are Ministers and Elders selected from the Synod in such number as the Synod deems necessary.

320. The official members of a Commission are a Moderator or Chairman and Clerk.

321. The Moderator and Clerk are appointed by the Synod. In the absence of the Moderator he appoints another member to discharge his duty.

Meetings.
322. The time and place of the first meeting of a Commission are usually fixed by the Synod. Subsequent meetings are held at such times and places as the Commission appoints.

Procedure.
323. The procedure of a Commission is regulated:—

(1) By the specific instructions of the Synod;
(2) by the forms and order of business followed in the Synod.

324. If a Commission is appointed only to take evidence in a case, it receives the evidence according to the rules stated in Section IX., Chapter X., and reports thereupon to next Synod.

325. If a Commission is appointed with full Synodical powers to decide a case which has come before the Synod, it proceeds therein according to the usual Synodical rules, and its decisions have the same authority and effect as those of the Synod.

326. A Commission must lay the record of all its proceedings before the next Synod.

CHAPTER IX.

RULES OF PROCEDURE COMMON TO ALL THE COURTS.

Section I.—Overtures.

327. An Overture is a proposal to the Synod,— Nature and design of an Overture.
   (*a*) either to declare, amend, enjoin, or repeal an existing law of the Church;
   (*b*) or, to enact a new law;
   (*c*) or, to introduce and pass any measure for the general benefit of the Church.

328. An Overture may proceed from a Presbytery, a Session, or a member or members of the Church. If an Overture be from a Session, it must be presented to a Presbytery for transmission to the Synod. If an Overture be from a member or members of a Congregation, it must be sent to a Presbytery by the Session of the Congregation to which the member or members belong for transmission to the Synod. If the Session refuse to transmit such Overture, the member or members who sent it have the right of appeal to the Presbytery. Origination and Transmission of an Overture.

329. A Presbytery may adopt and transmit an Overture to the Synod; or it may transmit an Overture from a Session or from a member or members of the Church *simpliciter*, that is, without expressing any opinion or judgment thereupon; or it may decline either to adopt or transmit an Overture.

330. Notice of intention to propose an Overture for transmission to the Synod by an Inferior Court must be given at a meeting of the Court previous to that at which the proposal is to be made. Notice of Overture.

331. All overtures transmitted must be accompanied with certified relative extract minutes, and be in the hands of the Synod Clerk at least ten days before the meeting of Synod. Minutes relative to Overtures.

332. When an Overture is presented to the Synod by the Committee on Bills and Business, it is read by the Clerk, and the member or members appointed, or the Par- Procedure of Synod upon an Overture.

ties entitled, to appear in support of it, are heard, subject to the pleasure of the Synod.

333. When an Overture from a Presbytery comes before the Synod, not more than two Members are heard in support of it. If there are several Overtures on substantially the same subject from different Presbyteries, only one Member from each Presbytery is heard in support of them.

334. A Member of Synod appointed by a Presbytery to support an Overture is not thereby constituted a party, and he is entitled to deliberate and vote upon the question raised by the Overture.

Section II.—References.

Matters of Reference.

335. An Inferior Court may refer any case, or any branch of a case, or some special point of difficulty connected with it, to the Superior Court, for advice, or for judgment.

Reference simpliciter.

336. The reference may be made *simpliciter*, that is, without the expression of any opinion or request on the part of the Inferior Court.

Procedure on making a Reference.

337. When an Inferior Court makes a reference it instructs its Clerk to transmit to the Clerk of the Superior Court all the documents and extract minutes connected with the matter referred; it appoints one or more of its Members to state the reference to the Superior Court; and it gives notice to the parties concerned in the reference that they are required to appear before that Court at its next meeting.

The immediate effect of a Reference.

338. By reference of a case, either *simpliciter*, or otherwise, from an Inferior Court to the Superior Court, all procedure in the case is stopped in the Inferior Court until the Superior Court has given its advice or judgment.

Rights of Members of a Court making a Reference.

339. Members of a Court by which a reference is made are not placed at the bar of the Superior Court when the reference is considered, and they have all their rights and privileges in that Court unimpaired.

Procedure on consideration of a Reference.

340. When a Superior Court takes up a case of Reference, the following order is observed:—

    1. All the documents connected with the Reference are read, and the member or members appointed to state the Reference and the grounds for making it are heard.

    2. Parties, if there be any, are heard.

3. The Court then considers, first, whether the Reference has come up in a formal manner, and, secondly, whether there were sufficient grounds for making it. If these two points are satisfactory, the Reference is sustained.

4. If the Reference is frivolous or unnecessary, or if it is brought up in an informal manner, it is dismissed.

5. If the Reference is sustained, and if it is one of importance and difficulty, the Court proceeds to deliberate, and to give such decision upon it as may seem proper. Its decision is intimated to the parties concerned in the case.

6. If the case is one which the Inferior Court itself should have carried to an issue, it may be sent back to that Court to proceed in it according to the rules of the Church.

Section III.—Dissents.

341. A Member of any Court who has voted on a Motion and is dissatisfied with the decision, may tender his Dissent and require it to be inserted in the Minutes. *Right of Dissent.*

342. A Dissent is not received and recorded unless given in immediately after the announcement of the decision dissented from. *Time for Dissent.*

343. Any Members present in Court when a Dissent is given in at the proper time may, at the time, or at the next meeting of the Court, intimate their adherence to that Dissent, and require that such dissent be recorded. *Adherence to Dissent.*

344. A Dissent may be either with or without reasons assigned. If reasons are assigned they must be put in writing, and either be given in along with the Dissent or be lodged in the hands of the Clerk of the Court within ten days thereafter. *Reasons of Dissent.*

[*See* 348, 349 *for procedure in Supreme Court.*]

345. Reasons, when given in along with a Dissent or afterwards, may be inserted in the Minutes or kept *in retentis*, according to the judgment of the Court. If reasons are inserted in the Minutes, the Court, if it deem necessary, prepares answers to them.

346. Any absent Member who has intimated to the Court a sufficient cause for his absence may dissent from a decision come to in his absence, either with or without reasons assigned, provided the Dissent be given in at the next Meeting of Court at which he is present. *Right of an absent Member to a Dissent.*

Limitation of the effect of a Dissent.	347. A Dissent does not entitle the Dissentient to bring the matter under the review of a Superior Court, nor does it give him a right to be heard on the matter should it afterwards come before the Superior Court.
Dissent in the Supreme Court.	348. In the Supreme Court a Member may dissent in his own name and also in the name of all who may signify their adherence to his Dissent, provided they have taken part in the vote by which the decision was come to, or were absent for sufficient cause.
	349. When a Dissent, with reasons assigned, is tendered in the Supreme Court, the reasons must be given in, in writing, either along with the Dissent, or at the session of the Court next following that at which the Dissent was tendered.

Section IV.—Complaints.

Dissent and Complaint.	350. A Member of an Inferior Court who has dissented from any of its judgments, may require that the judgment or judgments from which he dissents be carried before the Superior Court for review and decision. This procedure is technically known as Complaint, and a Member so acting is called a Complainant.
Time and Reasons for it.	351. A Complaint must be tendered immediately after the announcement of the judgment complained of, and be accompanied with reasons either given in, in writing, by the Complainant at the time, or lodged by him in the hands of the Clerk of the Court within ten days from the date of judgment.
Concurrence with a Complainant.	352. Other Members of the Court may intimate their concurrence with a Complainant, either for the reasons assigned by him, or for other reasons assigned by themselves, provided intimation of their concurrence is made at the time, or placed in the hands of the Clerk of the Court within ten days thereafter.

Section V.—Appeals.

Right of Appeal.	353. A Party in a case before an Inferior Court is entitled to Protest and Appeal against any of its judgments, and thereby require that the judgment or judgments against which he appeals be carried for review to the next higher Court. This procedure is technically known as Appeal. The Party so acting is called an Appellant.

354. An Appellant must tender his Appeal at the time that the judgment is announced, and he must give in reasons of Appeal, in writing, at the time, or lodge them in the hands of the Clerk of the Court within ten days thereafter. *Time and Reasons for Appeal.*

355. Reasons of Appeal may be such as these:—
Irregularity in the proceedings of the Inferior Court; Refusal of reasonable indulgence to a party in the conduct of the case; Reception of irrelevant evidence; Refusal to receive relevant evidence; Mistake or Injustice in the judgment; or, Undue haste in proceeding to judgment.

356. Members of a Court against whose judgment a Party appeals may become Complainants against the same judgment, as set forth in paragraph 352. *Right of Complaint.*

Section VI.—Procedure in Case of Complaint or Appeal.

357. The effect of a Dissent with Complaint, or of an Appeal, is to stay the action of the Court in the case, to carry the case to the Superior Court for review, and to hold the Complainants or the Appellants, and the Members of the Inferior Court bound to appear at the bar of the Superior Court when the case is called. *Effect of Complaint or Appeal.*

358. If an Inferior Court against whose judgment Dissent with Complaint, or Appeal, has been taken, considers the action of the Complainant or the Appellant frivolous or vexatious, it may disregard the Complaint or the Appeal, but does so at its own risk, the rights of the Complainant or the Appellant being always reserved. *Reservation of rights of Complainants or Appellants.*

359. A Court, against whose judgment Complainants or Appellants have duly tendered reasons, draws up answers to these reasons, either itself, or by a Committee appointed for the purpose, and appoints one or more of its Members to appear before the Superior Court in support of its judgment. *Answers to Reasons of Complaint or Appeal.*

360. The Court against whose judgment Complainants or Appellants have taken due proceedings, must send up all its records and all the papers in its possession relative to the case to the Superior Court. *Records and Papers in cases of Complaint or Appeal.*

361. Complainants and Appellants are entitled to such extracts from the minutes of the Inferior Courts, and to copies of such papers in the possession of these Courts, as are necessary to enable them to bring the subject of their Complaints or Appeals before the Superior Court. *Rights to Minutes and Papers in such cases.*

It is usual at the time of entering a Complaint or Appeal for such extracts to be craved and granted.

Instruction to Parties.

362. It is the duty of the Inferior Court to instruct Parties on the rules and forms of procedure applicable to their cases, when requested to do so, or when it is deemed necessary.

Procedure in cases of Complaint or Appeal.

363. A Superior Court before which Complainants or Appellants bring cases for review proceeds therein in the following order:—

    1. Calls for the Minutes of the Inferior Court and the Papers relative to the case, which are read.

    2. Calls the Parties in the case; who, in a case of Appeal or Complaint, are the Appellants or Complainants, and the Member or Members appointed to appear for the Inferior Court.

    3. Hears the Parties.

    4. Gives an opportunity to the Members of Court of putting questions to the Parties through the Moderator.

    5. Removes the Parties, considers the case, and proceeds to judgment.

    6. Recalls the Parties, and the Moderator intimates judgment to them.

    7. The Party in whose favour judgment is given expresses acquiescence, and craves extracts which are granted, and which he presents to the Inferior Court and on which that Court acts.

    8. The Members appointed to appear for the Inferior Court in the case receive a copy of the judgment given, which is laid before that Court at its next meeting.

Reference of a case of Complaint or Appeal to a Committee.

364. The Supreme Court may refer a case brought up by Appeal or Complaint to a Committee for consideration and report. In doing so, it must act with consent of all the parties, and with express reservation of all their rights. The proceedings of a Committee in such a case are in the order followed by the Court itself as stated in paragraph 363 so far as applicable. The Committee reports to the Court the decision to which it has come.

Decision on such a case.

365. The Court takes that decision into consideration and proceeds to judgment; but if any of the parties refuse to accept the decision of the Committee they are entitled to be heard by the Court itself before judgment is given.

Section VII.—Petitions.

366. The Courts of the Church receive and judge of Petitions or Memorials presented to them on matters connected with the doctrine, discipline, worship or government of the Church as a whole, or of any of its Congregations. — *Matters of Petition.*

367. Petitioners may be heard before the Courts to which their Petitions are presented. — *Petitioners.*

368. Petitions from individual members of the Church or from Congregations addressed to a Presbytery must pass through the Session, and Petitions addressed to the Supreme Court must pass through the Presbytery. — *Mode of transmitting Petitions.*

369. If an Inferior Court declines to transmit a Petition to a Superior Court, the Petitioner has the right of appeal, which proceeds in ordinary form.

370. An Inferior Court may address a Petition to the next Higher Court. — *Petition from a Court.*

371. When a Court finds that a Petition presented to it affects the interests and rights of other persons than the Petitioners, it directs that due notice thereof be given to such persons, and, if it sees fit, grants them an opportunity of being heard before giving a decision on the Petition. — *Persons affected by a Petition.*

Note referring to Sections II. to VII. in this Chapter.

Parties in a case of Reference, Dissent, Appeal, Complaint, or Petition, are not allowed to distribute papers bearing on the case to the Members of the Court before which the case comes.

CHAPTER X.

DISCIPLINE.

Section I.—Nature and Ends of Discipline.

Judicial.   372. Discipline is that exercise of the government of the Church which consists in the judicial administration of its laws.

373. Discipline is placed in the hands of those appointed to rule in the Church, and is exercised by them in their respective judicatories under the authority of the Lord Jesus Christ.

Spiritual.   374. Discipline is purely spiritual, and can only be applied within the spiritual province of the Church.

375. The ends of discipline are the glory of God, the condemnation of offences, the purity of the Church, and the spiritual good of offenders.

Section II.—Grounds for Discipline.

Offences.   376. Discipline is required by anything in the teaching or the conduct of those under the jurisdiction of the Church which (*a*) has been declared censurable by the Word of God, and by the law or practice of the Church founded thereon, and also (*b*) either gives rise, or may give rise, to scandal, or is manifestly injurious to the peace and purity of the Church.

377. In the case of an offence brought under the notice of a judicatory, which is not in itself heinous, and which has not created scandal, the ends of discipline respecting it may be attained, without entering on a judicial process, by private and fraternal dealing with the alleged offender on the part of members of the judicatory which has primary jurisdiction over him.

378. If an offence be heinous, and has given rise to scandal, or is fitted to give rise to scandal, it becomes a proper ground for discipline by a judicial process, and

the Court having primary jurisdiction over the alleged offender, ought to take steps for such process according to the rules of the Church.

379. An offence which has been unnoticed as a ground for discipline for five years should not be revived for the purposes of discipline unless it be heinous, or has recently become a cause of scandal.

SECTION III.—SUBJECTS OF DISCIPLINE.

380. The subjects of discipline are, in the first place, members of the Church in full communion; in the second place, members of the Church by Baptism, not in full communion, who have arrived at the years of discretion; and, in the third place, all other persons who have connected themselves with the Church. {Members and Office-bearers of the Church.}

381. The members of a Church Court are amenable to the discipline of the Court for offences against its order and authority committed during its sittings.

SECTION IV.—RAISING OF CHARGE OF OFFENCE.

382. No case of discipline is to be formally proceeded with until there has been fraternal dealing, on the part of the Court before which the case comes, by private conference with the alleged offender, with a view to avoid, if possible, the necessity of formal process. {Private dealing.}

383. A Court must not enter on a judicial process against an alleged offender unless some person or persons undertake to sustain the charge, or unless the Court itself find it necessary, for the ends of discipline, to investigate the alleged offence.

384. A Court must not enter on a formal process of discipline in a case of alleged personal and private injury, unless those means of reconciliation have been tried which are commanded by our Lord in Matthew xviii. 15-17. {Reconciliation.}

385. Any one bringing a charge of offence before a Court ought to give previous notice thereof to the party charged.

386. Any member of the Church bringing a charge against a fellow-member lightly or maliciously is himself guilty of a grave offence, and is liable to censure. {Bringing a charge.}

387. On the basis of public report of an offence, a Court may proceed to discipline to the extent of private dealing with the alleged offender, and of inquiry into the nature of the alleged offence, and the evidence available in proof of it. If the Court thereby finds that the alleged offence requires the exercise of discipline by a formal process, the Court itself charges the alleged offender with it in a judicial form, and proceeds with the case according to the rules of the Church.

Section V.—Statement of Charge.

Charge put in writing.

388. Whether the charge of an offence be brought before a Court by information, petition, or otherwise, or be made by a Court itself, the charge must be put in writing, setting forth the nature of the alleged offence, specifying, as far as possible, the time, place, and circumstances in which the offence is said to have been committed, and giving the names and designations of the witnesses, known and available, who are to be cited in support of the charge.

389. The Court may then, if it see fit, require a further statement, more or less detailed, according to circumstances, of the character of the evidence to be brought forward in the case.

Notice to alleged offender.

390. A Court receiving or making a charge in a case involving discipline, must transmit in writing, to the alleged offender, the particulars set forth in paragraphs 388 and 389.

A Court must at the same time inform the alleged offender that he has the right to cite witnesses in his defence, and require him, within a specified time, to send to the Clerk of the Court the names and designations of the witnesses known and available, to be cited in his defence.

Section VI.—Citation.

Parties. Witnesses.

391. A Court having resolved to proceed to trial in a case of discipline, must cite the following to appear before it, namely:—

    (1) The party making and prosecuting the charge, unless the Court itself be prosecuting the charge.

    (2) The party charged with the offence.

(3) The witnesses to be called at the instance of the party prosecuting.

(4) The witnesses to be called at the instance of the party charged.

392. A citation may be oral or written.

393. An oral citation is made by authority of the Court, by its Moderator or Clerk, when the parties or witnesses to be cited are present in Court. The fact of such citation must be recorded in the Minutes. *Oral citation.*

394. A written citation must run in the name of the Court, specify the time and place of the Meeting of Court at which the persons cited are to appear, set forth the nature of the charge to be tried, and be signed by the Moderator or Clerk of the Court. The fact of order having been given for such citation must be recorded in the Minutes. *Written citation.*

395. The time allowed, after citation, for the appearance of a party or witness, is determined by the Court with proper regard to the circumstances of the case, and must not be less than ten days *Service of citation.*

396. A written citation is duly served upon a party or witness when delivered to him personally by the hand of an officer authorised by the Court, or by registered letter addressed to him at his last known place of residence.

397. Members of the Church, when duly cited by a Court to appear either as parties or to give evidence in a case, are bound to obey the citation; and if they refuse after two citations, they are liable to be dealt with as contumacious, unless they offer satisfactory reason for non-appearance.

398. The citation of witnesses who are not members of the Church can only take the form of a request to them from the Court to appear and give evidence.

399. If a party in a case of discipline does not appear after being orally cited as above provided for, or after written citation duly served upon him twice to two several meetings of the Court, with not less than ten clear days between them, and without stating satisfactory reason for his non-appearance, the Court at the second of those meetings may treat him as a fugitive from discipline, hold him liable to censure for contumacy, and declare him no longer a member of the Church.

Section VII.—Procedure in Summary Trials.

Order of Procedure. 400. A Court met to consider the merits of a case of discipline, not needing an Indictment or Libel, but fully ripe for summary trial, proceeds in the following order:—

1. Announces specifically the charge made.
2. Calls the party making the charge. If the Court itself make the charge, it appoints one or more of its Members to act in support of it.
3. Calls the party charged.
4. Calls the witnesses (1) for the charge, (2) against it, and takes their evidence.
5. Hears the parties.
6. Gives a decision on the case.

Section VIII.—Procedure in Trial upon an Indictment.

Indictment. 401. In cases of very grave offence or heresy, a Court may find it necessary to proceed to a formal judicial trial upon an Indictment, or, as it has been hitherto commonly called, a Libel, against the alleged offender.

Form of Indictment. 402. An Indictment, fully drawn according to ancient ecclesiastical usage, consists of three parts forming a regular syllogism. The first, or major proposition, sets forth the nature of the offence charged, and declares it to be punishable according to the Word of God and the laws of the Church. The second, or minor proposition, asserts that the accused party is guilty of the offence charged, and narrates the facts involving his guilt, specifying time, place, and circumstances, in one or more distinct counts. The third proposition or conclusion, states the necessity for punishment, provided the accusation be found proven.

403. Great care ought to be taken in the framing of an Indictment. An Indictment incorrectly drawn, is not only unfair to the accused, if he is innocent, but is frequently his best protection if he is guilty.

The MAJOR PROPOSITION should be made as brief and comprehensive as possible. If more than one offence is included in the same Indictment, the different offences should be set forth separately in the major proposition, connected by the words "*as also.*" When aggravations of the offence charged are introduced into the Indictment, they should follow the statement of the offence to which they apply, preceded by the word "*especially.*"

The MINOR PROPOSITION ought to narrate the acts

which amount to the general offence set forth as punishable in the major. The narrative is introduced by the words "IN SO FAR AS." Where there are cumulative or alternative charges in the major proposition, the narrative in the minor should correspond. Accuracy and precision in setting forth the time, place, and circumstances of the alleged offence are essential in the minor proposition.

The CONCLUSION should follow logically from the major and minor propositions. It commences with the words, "ALL WHICH, or *part thereof, being* proven," etc.

According to modern usage an Indictment does not demand a specific punishment. The nature of the punishment is left to the Court before which the Indictment is brought and the case is tried.

[*See Specimen Form of Indictment in the Appendix.*]

404. A Court may proceed to trial at the instance of one or more persons presenting an Indictment against the accused, and undertaking to advance evidence in proof of it. — Presentation of Indictment.

405. A Court, on the basis of public *fama*, or information otherwise received, or on the basis of a petition, may, after preliminary investigation, and private dealing with an alleged offender, resolve to proceed by Indictment of its own accord.

406. When a Court of its own accord, or by direction of a Superior Court, resolves to proceed by Indictment, it appoints two or more of its Members to frame the Indictment, and lay it before the Court in their own name as prosecutors in the case.

The members appointed to draw up an Indictment may, if they see cause, consult the Synod's Committee on Judicial Procedure, or the legal Adviser of the Church, before submitting it to the Court.

407. A Court on receiving an Indictment signed by one or more prosecutors, after hearing it read, orders that a copy of it, attested by the Moderator or Clerk, be put into the hands of the accused, along with a list of the witnesses to be called in support of it, without prejudice to additional witnesses being afterwards brought forward, after due notice given. — Indictment put before the accused.

408. At the same time the Court, either there and then cites the accused, or orders that he be cited, to appear at a meeting to be held within not less than ten days, for the purpose of receiving any statement the accused may desire to offer at this stage, and of considering the relevancy of the Indictment, and the propriety of serving it upon him as the Indictment upon which he is to be tried. — Citation of the accused.

Relevancy of Indictment.

409. At the meeting held on the day appointed as in last paragraph the Court calls for the parties, hears any statement the accused may desire to offer, and then proceeds to consider the relevancy of the Indictment. The prosecutors are entitled to be heard in support of the relevancy, and the accused against it. If the accused be a member of the Court, he retains all the rights of a member while the question of relevancy is under consideration.

Relevancy of Indictment.

410. The relevancy of an Indictment includes two questions:

    1. Whether the offence charged in the major proposition is truly punishable according to the Word of God and the laws of the Church?

    2. Whether, if so, the facts alleged in the minor proposition, if proved, or admitted, would be sufficient to convict the accused of the offence charged, and render him liable to punishment?

Before deciding the question of the relevancy of an Indictment, the Court may, if it see cause, give leave to amend the Indictment.

Indictment dismissed.

411. If the Indictment be found irrelevant, it is dismissed, and the case takes end.

Procedure on relevant Indictment.

412. If the Indictment be found partly relevant and partly irrelevant, the Court may proceed on that part which is relevant.

413. Appeals, or Dissents and Complaints, on the question of the relevancy of an Indictment, do not stop procedure in the case; but judgment in the case is not given until these have been disposed of by a Superior Court.

414. When a Court has found an Indictment relevant, it asks the accused if he confesses the truth of the charge or charges set forth in the Indictment, and, if he confesses, it inflicts censure as required by the nature of the case and the rules of the Church.

415. If the accused deny the truth of the charge or charges in the Indictment, the Court resolves:—

    (*a*) That the Indictment, as found relevant, be served upon the accused party.

    (*b*) That the taking of evidence in the case be entered upon by the Court at an appointed time and place.

    (*c*) That all the parties be cited to appear at the meeting appointed for taking evidence.

    (*d*) That the accused, if a Minister in a Pastoral Charge, or a Professor of Theology, or a Missionary, be suspended from all the functions of his office until the case be finally adjudicated.

DISCIPLINE.

416. A Court met for taking evidence in a case of trial upon an Indictment observes the following order:— *Order followed.*

1. Calls the party by whom the Indictment has been laid. If the Indictment has been laid by the Court itself, it calls those members appointed to appear in support of it at the trial.

2. Calls the party indicted.

3. Calls the witnesses (1) for the Indictment, (2) against it, and takes their evidence, subject to cross-examination on both sides.

4. Directs that the evidence of witnesses be taken down in writing, be read over to them, and, if correct, be subscribed by them in the presence of the Clerk, or of a member of the Court appointed for the purpose.

5. Hears the parties in the case upon the evidence, (1) for the Indictment, (2) against it.

6. Proceeds to a decision on the case.

SECTION IX.—RULES OF EVIDENCE.

417. Witnesses are examined after a solemn affirmation administered to them by the Moderator. *Affirmation.*

[*See Specimen Form in Appendix.*]

418. Witnesses are first examined by the party producing them; then cross-examined by the opposite party; after which any member of the Court, or either party, may put additional questions. *Witnesses.*

419. The prosecutor and the accused, may, if either of them choose, give evidence on condition that they submit, like other witnesses, to cross-examination.

420. A Member of a Court, who is called upon to give evidence in a case, is not thereby disqualified from voting in it.

421. Hearsay is not valid evidence, unless it be corroborated. *Evidence.*

422. The unsupported evidence of one witness is not sufficient to establish a charge.

423. Circumstantial evidence is receivable.

424. Evidence of facts not pertinent to the issue is not admissible.

Evidence subscribed. 425. The evidence of witnesses is taken down in writing, is read over to them, and, if correct, is subscribed by them in the presence of the Clerk, or of a member of the Court appointed for the purpose.

If the evidence be taken in short-hand, a faithful transcript of it must be made, read over, and subscribed as stated above.

Evidence taken by a Commission. 426. When a Court finds it necessary to take the evidence in a case by a Commission, the Commission proceeds according to the rules followed by the Court itself, and lays the evidence in a complete and authentic form before the Court for its consideration and judgment.

427. The evidence of witnesses unable because of ill-health, old age, or other sufficient reason, to appear in Court or before a Commission, may be taken by a Committee of the Court or of the Commission, according to the rules followed by the Court itself, and, when so taken, is laid before the Court or the Commission as part of the evidence in the case.

Voting on evidence. 428. No member of the Court may vote as a judge in the case unless he has at least heard or read all the evidence on the side against which his vote is given.

Evidence laid before a Court of Appeal. 429. The evidence in a case, duly authenticated by the Moderator or Clerk of the Court by which it has been taken, is held as valid evidence by the Higher Court to which the case may be appealed.

New evidence and its effects. 430. If, after a trial before any Court, new evidence is discovered, alleged to be important to the exculpation of the accused, he may ask a new trial, and the Court may grant the request, if justice seem to require it; provided that if the Court be an Inferior one, and the case has been appealed from it, such application be made to the Higher Court.

431. If, in the prosecution of an appeal, new evidence is offered, which, in the judgment of the Higher Court, has an important bearing on the case, it may either refer the whole case to the Inferior Court for a new trial; or, with the consent of the parties, take the evidence, and then hear and determine the case.

Conflicting evidence. 432. When the evidence in a case is so conflicting that the Court cannot form an opinion either for or against the charge, it pronounces no judgment, and waits till the Providence of God throws further light on the case.

Section X.—Church Censures.

433. A Court having carried a judicial trial to a conclusion, and having found a charge proven, against which decision an appeal or complaint has not been taken, or, if taken, has been dismissed by a Superior Court, considers what sentence should be pronounced upon the offender, according to the nature and gravity of the offence. *Sentence.*

434. The sentences of the Court in such cases are called Church Censures. *Censures*

435. When a Court has determined the censure due in a case of discipline, it calls upon the offender to appear, and on his appearance, the censure is declared to him, in the name and in the presence of the Court, by the Moderator, who also addresses him in terms befitting the nature and circumstances of the case.

436. If the offender does not appear when called upon to receive censure, the censure is declared by the Moderator in his absence, and a copy of it and of the judgment upon which it followed is transmitted to him by the Clerk.

437. Church Censures are (*a*) Admonition, (*b*) Rebuke, (*c*) Suspension from the rights of Church membership or from the functions of Office, (*d*) Deposition from Office, (*e*) Removal from the Membership of the Church.

438. Admonition is the lowest degree of censure, and is a solemn address to an offender, setting his sin before him, and exhorting him to repentance and watchfulness. *Admonition.*

439. Rebuke is a higher degree of censure than Admonition, is administered to persons guilty of the graver offences, and is a solemn reproof of them in the name of the Lord Jesus Christ. *Rebuke.*

440. Suspension is a form of censure higher than Rebuke, and is a prohibition of the offender from exercising the rights of Church membership, or the functions of office in the Church. *Suspension*

441. Suspension is resorted to (*a*) when the offence requires a severer censure than Admonition or Rebuke, or (*b*) when, after Rebuke, the offender makes neither profession of repentance nor promise of amendment, or (*c*) when the offence is repeated.

442. Suspension is either for a specified or an unspecified time, according to the gravity of the offence and the circumstances of the case.

443. If an offender suspended from the rights of Church

membership be also an office-bearer, he is thereby also suspended from his office; and if his suspension be the act of a Superior Court, notice thereof must be given to the Inferior Court of which he is a member.

444. Suspension from office does not necessarily imply suspension from the rights of Church membership.

445. Suspension of a Minister from his office for a specified time does not, of itself, involve the dissolution of the pastoral tie between him and his Congregation, but such dissolution is involved in his Suspension from his office *sine die*.

446. Notice of the Suspension of a Minister is given to his Congregation by authority of the Court which passed the sentence.

Deposition.

447. Deposition is one of the highest forms of censure. It takes place only in the case of a Minister or Office-bearer, and consists in depriving him of his office in consequence of conviction or confession of some very grave offence, or of heresy.

Deprivation of Licence.

448. If a Licentiate be found guilty of some very grave offence, or of heresy, he is deprived of his Licence.

Contumacy.

449. In cases of contumacious resistance to the authority of the Courts of the Church, or of flight from discipline, and in cases of peculiar aggravation where the offence is obstinately denied, although fully proved, or, if acknowledged, is justified, and the offender continues impenitent, the offenders are declared no longer members or office-bearers of the Church.

SECTION XI.—REMOVAL OF CENSURES.

Cessation of Suspension.

450. Suspension for a specified time from the rights of Church membership, or from the functions of office, ceases at the expiration of the time specified, unless the Court which pronounced the censure see cause to remove it sooner.

Removal of Suspension.

451. Suspension for an unspecified time from the rights of Church membership, or from the functions of office, ought to be removed as soon as the Court which pronounced the censure is satisfied that the ends of discipline in the case have been attained.

452. In removing the Suspension of an offender from full communion or from office, the Court, before which he appears, by its Moderator, addresses him in terms ap-

propriate to the circumstances of the case, and declares him restored to full communion or to his office.

453. In the case of a Minister who has been suspended from his office *sine die*, the removal of the suspension does not restore him to his former pastoral charge, but only restores him to the exercise of his ministerial rights, and renders him eligible to a Call from a Congregation.

454. Deposition from office may be removed upon profession of repentance, followed by a course of consistent conduct; but, in the case of a Minister, only by the Supreme Court, or by a Presbytery acting under the direction of that Court. The removal of Deposition does not restore to office, but only restores to the exercise of ministerial rights. Removal of Deposition.

Restoration to office, after removal of Deposition, is dependent, in the case of Elders and Deacons, upon due election by a Congregation, and in the case of a Minister, upon a Call, carried out according to the rules of the Church.

455. A Probationer, whose Licence has been withdrawn, may have it restored upon profession of repentance borne out by a course of consistent conduct. Restoration of Licence.

456. The removal of censures is effected only by the Courts by which they were inflicted, or by other Courts acting under instruction of the Supreme Court. Courts.

457. The removal of the higher censures calls for great caution and prudence on the part of the Courts of the Church.

458. Offenders who have been subjected to discipline, and afterwards duly restored, ought to be received in their respective places in the Church with tender and brotherly regard. Reception of restored offenders.

Section XII.—Courts Administering Discipline.

459. The Courts by which discipline is administered are Sessions, Presbyteries, and Synod. Courts of Discipline.

460. No professional counsel is allowed to appear and plead in cases of trial before any of the Courts.

461. An accused person who feels unable to represent and plead his own cause with advantage may request and obtain leave for a Member of the Court to act with him and for him in the progress of the case. The Member so engaged is not allowed to vote in the case. Aid to accused.

Confession. 462. If, upon the accusation being made in Court, or at any later stage of a case, the accused confesses himself guilty of the offence charged, no further evidence is necessary, and the Court pronounces judgment according to the nature and circumstances of the offence.

463. A confession may be made orally, or in writing. If made orally, it must be reduced to writing, and then must be signed by the party making it as his free and voluntary confession, and be recorded in the Minutes of the Court.

A.—SESSIONS.

Limits of power. 464. A Session has power of discipline only within the Congregation under its jurisdiction.

465. Sessions have no power of discipline on Ministers or Probationers, who are subject only to the jurisdiction of the Higher Courts.

First steps in discipline. 466. A Session takes the first steps for the exercise of discipline over the members of a Congregation; but in the event of its neglect to take such steps, and in special cases, it may be directed to do so by a Superior Court.

467. A Session on receiving information of acts manifestly inconsistent with Christian conduct, but not of an aggravated character, on the part of a member of a Congregation, considers whether the purposes of discipline in such a case may be attained by dealing with him privately. See first, second, and third paragraphs in Sect. IV. of this Chapter.

If a Session decides in the affirmative, it appoints the Moderator, or more of its own number, to wait upon the member, to make inquiry, and thereafter to give admonition and counsel according to the best of their judgment in the case.

If this private action prove satisfactory, no further steps are taken.

Indictment. 468. In a case of discipline regarding an alleged offence of a flagrant character, on the part of a member or officebearer who does not admit his guilt, a Session proceeds by Indictment, according to the rules provided for that form of procedure in Section VIII. of this Chapter.

469. An Indictment must be presented by one or more persons acting as prosecutors, or by one or more members of the Session appointed to act as prosecutors.

470. In cases of special difficulty and importance, and in cases involving the highest censures of the Church, a Session before proceeding to trial, may, sometimes, with advantage, report them to the Superior Court, and request instructions as to further proceedings. — *Special cases.*

B.—PRESBYTERIES.

471. A Presbytery has power of discipline over its own Members, over the Congregations upon its Roll, and over the Probationers and Ministers without Pastoral Charge under its jurisdiction. — *Extent of power.*

Ministers without Pastoral Charge and Probationers are under the jurisdiction of the Presbytery which has recognised them as resident or labouring within its bounds.

If such recognition has not been given, they are under the jurisdiction of the Presbyteries by which they were licensed.

472. Judicial procedure in discipline in the case of a Probationer, Minister, Professor of Theology, or Missionary, can be entered upon only by the Presbytery which has jurisdiction over him, and can be so entered upon either in virtue of its own authority, or of special direction given to it by the Supreme Court.

473. The exercise of discipline by a Presbytery on Elders, Deacons, and Members of the Church is, in ordinary practice, limited to cases brought before it from Sessions by Reference, Appeal, or Complaint. — *Cases from Sessions.*

474. When a Presbytery proceeds to the trial of a case upon an Indictment, it observes the methods of procedure stated in Section VIII. in this Chapter. — *Indictment.*

475. When a Presbytery, in a case of procedure upon Indictment of a Minister, Professor of Theology, or Missionary, has formally served the Indictment upon him, he is thereby suspended from the exercise of all the functions of his office until the case shall be finally adjudicated, either by the Presbytery itself, or, if an appeal has been taken, by the Supreme Court. — *Suspension following Service of Indictment.*

Such Suspension is not of the nature of a censure, but is an act rendered necessary by the position of one publicly charged with an offence for which he has been put on trial.

476. If a Minister suspended from office during his trial upon Indictment be in a Pastoral Charge, the Presbytery notifies the Suspension to his Congregation,

appoints a Moderator of Session in his room, and makes suitable arrangements for the supply of his pulpit while the Suspension lasts.

Right to call for an Indictment.
477. If a Minister feels himself aggrieved or injured by the circulation of charges seriously affecting his teaching or conduct, he is entitled to require his Presbytery to set forth these charges in the form of a regular Indictment, before he is called upon to make any statement respecting them.

Reference to Supreme Court.
478. It is competent to a Presbytery, after having served an Indictment upon a Minister, if it see cause, to refer the case to the Supreme Court of the Church.

This reference is not to be made except in cases of special difficulty or importance. It may be made either on the ground that it does not appear expedient, in the circumstances, for the Presbytery to act both as prosecutors and judges, or on the ground that it does not appear expedient, in the circumstances, for the proof to be taken except before the Court which has the power of giving a final deliverance in the case.

Direction to a Session.
479. A Presbytery has power to direct a Session to originate a process of discipline on office-bearers or members under its jurisdiction, and carry it on according to the rules of the Church.

Communication from one Presbytery to another.
480. If an offence alleged against a Probationer or a Minister without Pastoral Charge be declared to have been committed within the bounds of another Presbytery than that to which he belongs, and be brought by *fama*, or otherwise, under the notice of the Presbytery within whose bounds it is declared to have been committed, it is the duty of that Presbytery to communicate the information which it has received to the Presbytery which has jurisdiction over the alleged offender, in order that it may proceed according to the rules of the Church.

C.—The Synod.

Extent of power.
481. The Synod, as the Supreme Court of the Church, has power of discipline co-extensive with the Church.

482. In ordinary practice the Synod exercises its power of discipline only in cases brought before it from Inferior Courts by Reference, Appeal, or Complaint.

483. In such cases the Synod observes the rules applicable to References, Appeals, and Complaints on other matters.

484. If the question brought up to the Synod be as to the Relevancy of an Indictment against a Probationer, Minister, or Professor of Theology, and the Synod find the Indictment irrelevant in whole or in part, the Synod, if it see fit, may give leave to amend the Indictment and direct the Inferior Court to proceed in the case upon the amended Indictment. *Relevancy of Indictment.*

485. If the question brought before the Synod be as to the judgment of the Inferior Court upon the merits of the case, the Synod proceeds upon the evidence laid before the Inferior Court duly authenticated and transmitted by the Clerk thereof, and upon the pleadings at the bar. See 416. *Judgment. Evidence.*

486. When the Synod enters on the merits of a case of Indictment brought from an Inferior Court it observes the order set forth in Section VIII. in this Chapter. *Procedure.*

487. When the Synod remits a case of discipline to a Commission it either gives special instructions to the Commission as to the nature and limits of its procedure in the case, or it gives the Commission full power to carry the case to an issue upon its merits, according to the rules of the Church. *Case sent to a Commission.*

In all cases the Commission reports its action to the next Synod.

488. When, in a case of Indictment against a Probationer, the judgment of the Synod is Deprivation of Licence; or, if against a Minister, is Suspension, or Deposition, from Office; the Synod either itself pronounces the sentence, or directs that it be pronounced by the Presbytery from which the case has come up. *Pronouncing of Sentence.*

489. In the case of a charge of very grave offence or heresy raised against a Missionary on the Foreign Field who is not on the Roll of a Presbytery of the Church, the originating of procedure belongs to the Synod, which may appoint a Special Commission to investigate and try the case, or direct a Presbytery to do so, according to the rules of the Church. *Case of a Missionary.*

APPENDIX.

A.—STANDING ORDERS OF SYNOD.

1. That for the convenience of Sessions the Clerk shall, at least one month before the meeting of Synod, issue to each Session a copy of the form of Commission, and of the Certificate appointed to be used for certifying Elders.

2. That all Commissions transmitted to the Clerk of Synod shall be revised by him, in so far as regards the regularity of said Commissions in point of form, and that he shall report to the Committee appointed by the Synod for revising Commissions only such as are defective or irregular.

3. That all Overtures, Returns to Overtures from Inferior Courts, and all papers transmitted by the Inferior Courts shall be in the form of Certified Extracts from the Minutes of said Courts, and that all such, as well as Elders' Commissions, shall be in the hands of the Clerk of Synod ten days at least before the meeting of Synod.

4. That papers in cases from Inferior Courts, whether forming part of the Record or produced in evidence before said Courts, shall, in each case, before they are given in, be duly dated, numbered, and initialled by the Clerk of the Court from which they come, and be accompanied by petition for transmission to the Committee on Bills by the parties sending them in.

5. That the Synod at its first Sederunt shall appoint two Committees—one to be called the Committee on Commissions and Records, and the other the Selection Committee. That the former shall consist of forty members, all chosen by the Synod; and it shall be charged with the revision of such Elders' Commissions as the Clerk may report to be defective or irregular, and of the Records of the Synod, the Presbyteries, and the Standing Committees. That the latter shall consist of the Conveners of existing Standing Committees, along with a member selected by each Presbytery—his name to be forwarded to the Clerk ten days before the meeting of Synod; and

that it shall be charged with the nomination of suitable persons to act on the various Committees of the Church.

6. That on the appointment of any Committee to do work during the sittings of Synod, a notice containing the names of the members shall be posted up in the porch immediately after their first announcement in Synod.

7. That at a suitable time the Synod shall appoint a Committee on Bills and Business for the following Synod; that it shall be chosen jointly by the Synod and the Presbyteries—each Presbytery being authorised to nominate one member for every fifteen congregations or fraction thereof—the names of the persons so nominated to be in the hands of the Clerk ten days before the meeting of the said following Synod; that it shall be charged with the revision and transmission of all papers to be laid on the table of the Synod, and with the arrangement of the Order of Business; and that it shall meet on the afternoon of the day of the Synod's meeting, so as to be able to report at the first Sederunt.

8. That the Synod shall meet on Monday evening at Six o'clock, and shall be prepared to enter on business not later than Eight o'clock.

9. That the Clerk shall report to the Synod on the Monday evening in regard to Elders' Commissions, so that the Roll may be made up at once, except in the case of such defective or irregular Commissions as may have been reported to the Committee on Commissions and Records.

10. That the following arrangements shall, as far as practicable, be observed during the sittings of the Synod, namely:—

MONDAY.

    1. That the Business Committee shall submit its Report immediately after that on Ministerial Changes, to be followed by—
- (*a*) Applications from Persons and Places.
- (*b*) Petitions, References, and other Communications *not* cognate to Reports of Synodical Committees.
- (*c*) Such other Business as the Business Committee may suggest.

TUESDAY.

    1. That the Synod shall first observe the ordinance of the Lord's Supper—the service not to extend beyond an hour—and then proceed to business, without adjournment.

2. That immediately after the reception of the Reports of the Committee on defective or irregular Commissions (if any), the Corresponding Members of the United Presbyterian Church, the Free Church of Scotland, and the Calvinistic Methodist Church in Wales, be received by an official recognition from the Moderator's Chair, with a brief reply from one of the Corresponding Members of each Church; after which the reports of the Business and Selection Committees shall be received.

3. That one hour thereafter be devoted to the reception of the Reports of Synod Deputies, after which the morning sitting to be devoted, as far as necessary, to the Reports of the Home, Jewish, and Foreign Missions.

4. That the Missionary Meeting in the evening commence at Seven o'clock, the preceding hour being occupied with minor pieces of business, as may be arranged by the Business Committee.

WEDNESDAY.

1. That the Report of the College Committee shall immediately follow that of the Committee on Ministerial Support, the remainder of the Sederunt being occupied by such other business as may be arranged.

2. That the reception of Deputies from other Churches shall form an order of the day for 7.30 in the evening, the preceding hour and a half being devoted to General Business; that no Deputy be heard who has not been formally commissioned; that the papers of Deputies, having been duly passed through the Business Committee, be simply reported but not read in court; that Deputies from Home Churches be received first, and then those from Colonial and Foreign Churches, the two latter changing places at alternate Synods; that not more than two Deputies be heard from any one Church; that each Foreign Deputy be allowed a quarter of an hour, provided the whole of the Foreign Deputies do not in any case occupy more than one hour in all; and that the Moderator acknowledge the addresses of the Deputies at the close without formal motion.

THURSDAY.

1. That the morning be reserved, as far as possible or necessary, for important questions that may from time to time be brought before the Synod.

2. That Committees to which matters shall have been specially referred submit their Reports, as far as possible, in the evening up till 7.30 [or 8] o'clock,

when there shall be an order of the day for the reception of the Report on the Instruction of Youth.

FRIDAY.
That this day shall be devoted to the remanent business of the Synod, and that Members shall be expected to arrange to remain over the day.

11. That, except in the case of the last day's proceedings, the Minutes, having been previously printed and placed in the hands of Members, shall be held as read, and be sustained accordingly at the beginning of each day's proceedings, with such corrections as may then be made.

12. That the Reports of the Committees of the Synod shall be printed and circulated along with the Minutes of Synod; and that a copy of the same shall be bound up in volumes and preserved among the Documents of the Synod.

13. That in cases where parties are called to the bar, two speeches only shall be heard from each party, including the reply, to which the appellant or complainant shall be entitled. But if there be more than two parties, there shall be only one speech from each, besides the reply. In case of there being more than one complainant, and it appearing that the complaints are on distinctly separate grounds, each may be considered a separate party.

14. That the following shall be the order in regard to Motions, Votes, and Decisions :—(1) Every motion or amendment shall be given in to the Clerk, in writing, as soon as it shall have been read to the House. (2) When a motion is duly seconded, and in possession of the Synod, it shall not be competent to make any alteration upon it without the permission of the House, except as an amendment thereon, or as an alternative motion, as the case may be, regularly proposed to the Synod. (3) The person who makes the first motion shall be entitled to the privilege of giving a reply, in which new matter must not be introduced; thereafter, the debate shall be held definitively closed, and no other person shall be entitled to speak, excepting in regard to the manner of putting the vote. (4) When there are only two motions before the House the question put to the vote shall be—Motion or Amendment, or first or second Motion ? When there are more than two Motions a vote is taken successively upon each, and unless it shall appear that one of the Motions has a clear majority of all the votes, that which had the least number shall be dropped, and a fresh vote taken upon those that remain, till only one shall be left,

when the remaining Motion shall be finally put to the House as a substantive Motion—provided always that—
(5) In the course of any discussion, a member may move a Resolution that *the question under consideration shall not be put;* in which case, so soon as the mover of the Resolution shall have explained the reasons on account of which he proposes it, the vote upon it shall be forthwith taken, such Resolution taking precedence of every other Motion before the House, and, should it be carried, the business shall immediately take end. (6) The voting shall be either by an open show of hands or by ballot, or by calling the Roll of the House. In the first case the Moderator or Clerk counts the votes, but if needful, tellers may be appointed to assist him. In the case of ballot, voting papers shall be prepared and supplied to Members of the Court; and on their being collected they shall be referred to two or more scrutineers appointed by the Court, who shall ascertain the result and report the same. In the case of calling the Roll, the names of the members arranged in Presbyteries are called seriatim by the Clerk, and each Member's vote on being tendered is marked by the Clerk. The votes are then summed up, and the result announced by the Moderator.

15. That in bringing up a Report from the Committee, the Convener thereof shall move the reception of the Report, and the adoption of such Resolutions as the Report contains or suggests, may be proposed to the House, with such additional Resolution or Resolutions as may seem necessary or desirable.

16. That any proposal for a pause in the Synod's proceedings, with a view to engage in special Devotional Exercises, shall be made to the Synod only through the Moderator. That all letters addressed to the Moderator for the purpose of being communicated to the House shall, in the first instance, be laid before the Business Committee, who shall advise the Moderator on the way of disposing of them.

17. That the Records of Synod, Presbyteries, and Standing Committees be called for at the first Morning Sitting, and remitted to the Committee on Records for examination. The Moderator or Clerk shall attest the same in accordance with their report.

18. That no Committee shall continue to sit after the Moderator shall have taken the Chair.

B.—SUSTENATION FUND ACT, 1879.

I.

That the Committee charged with securing a minimum stipend for this Church be designated the Sustentation Committee, and the Fund raised for this purpose the Sustentation Fund.

II.

That the Sustentation Committee take such steps as may be necessary for securing the formation of a special organization in each Congregation of the Church for the support of the Sustentation Fund, such special organization being hereinafter described as the Sustentation Fund Association; and that the Committee use every prudent and constitutional means to bring the practice of all the Congregations, with respect to the support of the Ministry and maintenance and use of the Fund, into as uniform a state as practicable.

III.

That each Congregation make a return to the Committee of the amount raised by the Sustentation Fund Association distinct from ordinary revenue.

IV.

That Congregations shall be placed on the equal dividend platform, when the sums they severally propose to contribute to the Sustentation Fund shall have been approved by the Presbytery of the bounds and the Committee. Further, that a re-arrangement be made with every Congregation on its becoming vacant, and that no step shall be taken for the filling up of the vacancy till this shall have been done.

V.

That the following be the regulations in regard to aid-receiving Congregations, viz.:—

1. That no Congregation be placed on the equal dividend platform unless it agrees to remit to the Fund at least one half of the equal dividend.

2. That Congregations which in the judgment of the Committee occupy positions in which they might fairly be expected to be self-sustaining, shall not have a claim to be on the equal dividend platform as aid-receiving unless under special instructions from the Synod.

3. That every Congregation shall be required to send up to the Central Fund, in addition to what is raised by its

Association, the proceeds of all church-door collections for support of ordinances, together with the seat-rents, after paying the usual Congregational expenses.*

4. That the organization in any Congregation be not deemed satisfactory till—

(1) A periodical opportunity is afforded to the Congregation of contributing to the Fund through its Association, which it is desirable should, if possible, be monthly;

(2) A large percentage on the membership are contributors;

(3) The total amount paid in to the Central Fund from all sources reaches a minimum of 12s. per annum on the membership, of which sum it is desirable that not less than a ratio of one penny per week on the membership be raised by the Association.

5. That it be not lawful for any such aid-receiving Congregation to pay to their Minister a supplement.

6. That Congregations obtaining grants from the Lady Hewly Trust, or other sources, which cannot be paid in to the Sustentation Fund, shall after correct returns have been made to the Committee, receive the equal dividend, minus the amount of such funds, in so far as they go towards the Minister's stipend; the object of the Sustentation Fund being not to supersede such special sources of revenue, but to raise the total income of Ministers to a given minimum stipend.†

---

* The Sustentation Fund Committee have resolved:—
I.—To allow as legitimate charges on the ordinary income of Congregations—
    1. The cost of Communion elements.
    2. The Presbytery's assessment of Congregations for Presbytery expenses.
    3. The Synod's assessment of Congregations for Synod Fund.
    4. A reasonable amount for ministers' travelling expenses to ordinary meetings of Presbytery, where not provided for in Presbytery expenses.
II.—Not to allow as legitimate charges on ordinary income of Congregations—
    1. Allowances to Ministers at Communions other than the cost of Communion elements.
    2. The cost of repairs of Church, except of a trifling character.
    3. Rents of Ministers' houses.
    4. Interest on debt of Manses.

† The Synod of 1893 resolved as follows:—
"Regarding the Congregations remaining on the Lower Platform, the Synod resolve that the Hewley Grant shall not be reckoned as part of the dividend of any Minister whose stipend together with such grant does not exceed the amount of the equal dividend."

7. That the Synod determine each year the number of charges to be raised to the platform of the equal dividend in the course of the ensuing twelve months, so as to obviate the risk of the Fund's being subjected to an undue pressure in any one year, and the consequent sudden depression of the equal dividend.

8. That in the event of any Congregation failing to fulfil its engagement towards the Fund, the Committee shall deal with that Congregation directly, and through the Presbytery, and, if necessary, bring the case before the Synod, which shall, if it see cause, remove the Congregation from the equal dividend platform.

9. That all aid-receiving Congregations not on the equal dividend platform be dealt with by the Sustentation Fund Committee, so as most effectually to develop their respective resources, by means of a direct grant on a given basis to make up a certain amount, and an additional grant of one-half more on any increase of their contributions until the amount of the equal dividend is reached; but that such additional grant shall be subject to the same limitation as applies to the equal dividend, that no Congregation shall receive more than double the sum remitted by it. Further, that all contributions toward stipend be sent to the Sustentation Fund, as in the case of other aid-receiving Congregations.

10. That in the event of Congregations becoming vacant whose contributions have not yet become sufficient to enable them to be placed upon the equal dividend platform, no new settlement shall take place without the due consideration by the Presbytery of the bounds of the necessity for retaining such Congregations in the position of separate and regular charges, nor, in the event of their judging this to be necessary, without the concurrence of the Sustentation Fund Committee in that judgment; cases of difficulty to be referred to the Synod.

11. That in the event of the occurrence of a vacancy in an aid-receiving Congregation situated in the immediate neighbourhood of one or more other Congregations, the Presbytery within whose bounds such Congregation is situated shall not proceed to a settlement of a new Minister without prior consultation and agreement with the Sustentation Committee in regard to the necessity for retaining such Congregation as a separate and independent charge, and, if it shall seem expedient, the use of all prudent means to effect a union between the vacant Congregation and a neighbouring one; cases of difficulty to be referred to the Synod.

12. That every Congregation be required to furnish the Committee with an annual statement of its accounts duly certified by the Presbytery of the bounds.

VI.

That the following be the regulations in regard to self-sustaining and aid-giving Congregations, viz. :—

1. That the minimum contributions from all sources which such Congregations shall be expected and encouraged to send to the Sustentation Fund, be adjusted by negotiation between the Committee and each Congregation, subject to the sanction of the Presbytery, on a common basis applicable to the whole Church.

2. That so long as the proceeds of Sustentation Fund Associations fall short of the sum so fixed, Deacons' Courts and Committees of Management be urged to make a payment to the Fund out of their ordinary revenue.

3. That said payment do not exceed in any case the amount of the equal dividend, but shall be subject on the other hand to all reasonable deductions, as, for example, where local revenue has fallen off since the Sustentation Fund has been started, or where exceptionally heavy charges of any kind fall upon local funds.

4. That in seeking to bring Congregations into harmony with those arrangements, the Committee shall deal in detail with the circumstances of each case, and shall make its appeal only to the generosity and sense of duty to the whole Church which ought to characterise all our people.

5. That where Congregations simply send the proceeds of Associations or other contributions to the Fund without receiving the equal dividend from it, but pay their ministers their entire stipends out of their Congregational funds, said payment shall be duly reported to the Committee, and the Congregations credited and debited in the Committee's books with the amount of the equal dividend.

6. That where, on the other hand, the Minister participates in the equal dividend, but receives in addition a supplement out of the Congregational funds, Congregations be recommended, in the case of future settlements, in order to avoid complication from the rise or fall of the equal dividend, to make their arrangements so that the total stipend shall be understood to consist of the equal dividend *plus* the supplement allowed, the fixed sum being thus the amount of supplement rather than the total stipend.

VII.

That any surplus beyond the minimum stipend aimed at be distributed in such a way as to stimulate Congregations to an increase of contributions to the Sustentation Fund.

VIII.

That Presbyteries shall not grant moderation in a Call to a Colleague in the case of any Congregation receiving aid from the Sustentation Fund without consultation and agreement with the Sustentation Committee, with a view to the protection of the interests of the Fund; cases of difficulty to be referred to the Synod. Further, that in the case of collegiate charges on the equal dividend platform, one dividend only be paid to each.

IX.

That all Church Extension charges which require extraordinary aid for a time, be placed under the care of the Home Mission Committee, until the period for such aid expire; that they then be dealt with by the Sustentation Fund Committee according to the foregoing regulations.

X.

That donations and legacies be solicited for the Fund.

C.—FUND FOR AGED AND INFIRM MINISTERS.

Rules as approved by the Synod in 1881-2.

1. That this Fund shall be for the benefit of (1) Ministers who have held a charge, (2) Missionaries who have laboured in connection with the Missions of this Church, and who shall, through ill-health or old age, have become permanently incapacitated for duty.

2. That applications shall be made (1) on behalf of a Minister, by the Presbytery of which he has been a member, and (2) on behalf of a Missionary, by the Committee under which he has laboured, and shall be accompanied, in each case, by a medical certificate; further, that all applications shall be made through the Committee in charge of the Fund, and reported on by it to the Synod, with which alone the final decision shall rest.

3. That loss of ecclesiastical status, as also emigration (except on medical advice), or the undertaking employ-

ment which, with the amount of the grant made from this Fund, would yield an income exceeding £150, shall terminate the claim of the annuitant; but that in the last case the Committee shall have power to make a grant that would raise the total income of the annuitant to a sum not exceeding that named, and also to replace the annuitant on the Fund in the event of the loss of such income. Further, that this Fund shall not be available to those who are already annuitants on the corresponding fund of any other Church.

4. That any Minister or Missionary, having reached the age of seventy, shall be exempt from the requirement of a medical certificate.

5. That the Committee in recommending grants shall have respect to the length of the Minister's or Missionary's service; and that the maximum grant shall be meanwhile £45 per annum.

6. That payment shall only be made out of revenue, and should this prove at any time insufficient, shall be made *pro rata*.

7. That it shall be free to annuitants on this Fund to apply for an annuity from the Pirie Trustees, according to the rules of that trust, but that their acceptance as annuitants by said Trustees shall terminate their claim on this Fund.

8. That Congregations be permitted to make such additional allowances as they may be able to do, out of their own funds, subject, in the case of Congregations receiving aid from the Sustentation Fund, to the approval of the Committee on Ministerial Support, and on the understanding that their contributions to the Sustentation Fund shall not be diminished thereby.

D.—MINISTERS' WIDOWS' AND ORPHANS' FUND.

INSTITUTED 1870.

Rules as amended by the Synod in 1884, 1885, 1891, *and* 1892.

CONSTITUTION OF THE FUND.

1. There shall be a Capital Fund formed from donations, legacies, annual rates, subscriptions, occasional collections, and any other available sources. — Capital.

Membership.

2. The membership of the Fund shall consist of Ministers, Professors, and Missionaries of the Church.

3. The ordinary rate of contribution shall be £5 per annum.

4. A double rate shall be payable by Foreign Missionaries and by members residing within a tropical climate. But Foreign Missionaries sent out by the Church may be on the Fund on the same terms as Ministers at home, provided that the Foreign Missions Committee shall, plus the Missionary's contribution, make an equal payment on his account.

5. Any member passing into another profession or into the service of another Church shall pay a special rate of £7 10s. per annum.

6. In the case of Ministers inducted into charges in the Church who have come from Churches other than those with which relations of mutual eligibility are established, any such Minister who is above the age of thirty at the time of his induction shall be chargeable on his settlement with an amount equal to what he would have been required to pay to this Fund had he been settled at that age, together with interest on that amount at 5 per cent., payable by double rates, till the whole amount has been made up.

7. From and after the adoption of this scheme, every one inducted to a Ministerial Charge or to a Professorship shall be required to connect himself with the Fund, and to continue his connection with it so long as he shall retain his Charge or Professorship, his first half-yearly payment being due at the first half-yearly term (of April 1 or October 1) next after his induction, he being entitled to the privileges of Membership from the date of his induction.

8. The rate shall be payable half-yearly, on April 1 and October 1, and any member failing to forward his contribution within one month after the date at which it is due shall be held to have forfeited his interest in the Fund.

9. On the occasion of each induction, the Congregation shall be required to contribute a sum of not less than 2 per cent. on the first year's stipend which the Minister is to receive.* The College Committee shall be required to make a similar contribution on the appointment of

---

* If a similar fee has been paid within five years, Congregations shall be exempt from the payment required by this rule, provided the Minister inducted is already a member of the Fund.

each Professor, and the Foreign Missions Committee on that of each Missionary.

10. (a) When a member of the Fund shall marry, he shall pay a fee of £5. If the age exceed that of his wife by more than seven years, the fee payable shall be according to the following scale:—

Member's Age.	Wife's Age.				
	Exceeding 7 Years but not exceeding 10 Years Younger.	Exceeding 10 Years but not exceeding 15 Years Younger.	Exceeding 15 Years but not exceeding 20 Years Younger.	Exceeding 20 Years but not exceeding 25 Years Younger	Exceeding 25 Years Younger.
	£	£	£	£	£
Not exceeding 40	6	11	24	31	40
,, 45	7	13	28	40	49
,, 50	8	21	33	43	58
,, 55	10	30	47	62	67
,, 60	15	35	54	71	85
,, 65	17	42	70	90	113
Exceeding 65	19	48	78	103	125

Such fees shall be payable, half at the half-yearly term next after marriage, the remainder one year later.

(b) Should the member fail to pay the marriage fee as specified above, and the amount not be made up with interest at 5 per cent. per annum in any other way, the Annuity payable to his widow shall be according to the following reduced scale:—

Member's Age.	Wife's Age.				
	Exceeding 7 Years but not exceeding 10 Years Younger.	Exceeding 10 Years but not exceeding 15 Years Younger.	Exceeding 15 Years but not exceeding 20 Years Younger.	Exceeding 20 Years but not exceeding 25 Years Younger.	Exceeding 25 Years Younger.
	£	£ s.	£ s.	£ s.	£ s.
Not exceeding 40	28	27 0	24 0	21 0	19 0
,, 45	24	22 0	20 0	18 0	16 0
,, 50	20	17 0	16 0	15 0	13 10
,, 55	16	14 0	12 10	11 10	11 0
,, 60	13	11 0	10 0	9 0	8 8
,, 65	11	9 0	8 0	7 0	6 10
Exceeding 65	10	7 10	6 10	5 10	5 0

(c) This rule shall apply to a Probationer who has been married before his ordination, in which case the fee shall be payable by two equal yearly instalments, the first being due at the half-yearly term next after his ordination, and the second a year after.

11. If a member shall die before he has paid into the Fund an amount equal to the annuity of a widow for two years, and such amount shall not be made up in any other way, a sum equal to his annual rate shall be deducted year by year from the annuities due, until such amount shall, by the payments made by the deceased in his lifetime and by subsequent deductions, have been made good to the Fund.

Annuities Fund.

12. The portion of the annual revenue available for annuities shall be the entire interest of the capital for the time being, together with not more than 70 per cent. of the subscriptions of members for the year.

MANAGEMENT.

13. The administration of the Fund shall be in the hands of a Committee appointed by the Synod.

14. The Committee shall lay before the Synod at the Ordinary Annual Meeting a full Report of their accounts and transactions throughout the year.

PRINCIPLES AND RULES OF ADMINISTRATION.

Recipients.

15. The beneficiaries of the Fund shall be the widows and children of deceased members who have fulfilled the requirements of the Fund.

Annuities.

16. The annuity payable to a widow shall be £30. The annuity shall cease in the event of her marrying again.

17. The annuity payable to orphans shall be £10 each; the annuity to cease on their reaching the age of eighteen years.

18. Should the orphan or orphans be motherless at the father's death, the annuity shall be increased to £15.

19. Annuities shall be payable half-yearly, on the first day of April and the first day of October. The first half-yearly payment shall be made at the term next after the death of the member; the last to a widow, at the term immediately preceding her re-marriage or death; and the last to a child, at the term immediately preceding its death, or attainment at the age of eighteen years. There shall be no payment for any part of a half-year.

20. Annuitants are required to produce the following certificates, viz.:—

 (*a*) Certificate as to the death of the Minister, Professor, or Missionary, and the date thereof.

 (*b*) Certificate attesting that the widow is alive, and remains unmarried.

(c) Certificate as to the existence of children under eighteen years of age.

(d) Certificates as to the dates of the said children's births.

21. These rules are not to make any contract, legal or equitable; and annuitants shall not have any claim against the officials of the Synod, or against the ratepayers, or against the Committee of Management, or against the trustees, either individually or collectively; nor is any personal liability incurred by those engaged in administering the Fund. Responsibility.

PERIODICAL REVISION.

22. There shall be a revision of the state of the Fund every three years, and no change shall be made in the rates or annuities except on actuarial advice and by Synodical authority.

ANNUAL AUDIT.

23. There shall be a yearly audit of the accounts by a professional accountant, who shall also examine the securities, and send to the Committee, through the Treasurership Committee, a valuation of the same as on the thirty-first day of December each year.

E.—HOME MISSION.

RULES AS AMENDED, 1887 AND 1890.

I.—ORGANIZATION OF COMMITTEE AND DISTRICT BOARDS.

1. That, without interfering in any way with the rights, powers, and jurisdiction of the Presbyteries, the Home Mission Work of the Church be conducted in future by a General Committee, to be called the General Home Mission Committee, together with three District Boards, to be called District Home Mission Boards.

2. That with this view the Presbyteries of the Church be grouped in three districts as follows :—

(a) The Southern District, embracing the Presbyteries of London North and South, and Bristol.

(b) The North-Western and Midland District, embracing the Presbyteries of Liverpool, Manchester, Carlisle, and Birmingham.

(c) The North-Eastern District, embracing the Presbyteries of Newcastle, Northumberland, Berwick, and Darlington.

3. That the General Home Mission Committee shall consist of eighteen members, appointed by the Synod (whom the Selection Committee shall be instructed to nominate in future in equal proportions from the three districts named, and with special regard to fitness), one-third to retire annually after the third year, but to be eligible for re-election; together with the Presbytery representatives.

4. That each District Board shall consist of the six local members of the General Home Mission Committee synodically appointed, of an equal number of the Presbytery representatives, especially designated to this duty by the respective Presbyteries, and of such number of local associates, not fewer than twelve, as the twelve thus directly appointed shall deem it advisable to add to their number from the membership of the Church within the district. Further, that the number to be specially designated by the several Presbyteries for their respective District Boards shall be meanwhile—

(a) Southern District—London, 5; Bristol, 1; total, 6.
(b) North-Western and Midland—Liverpool, 2; Manchester, 2; Carlisle, 1; Birmingham, 1; total, 6.
(c) North-Eastern—Newcastle, 3; Northumberland, 1; Berwick, 1; Darlington, 1; total, 6.

5. That the convener of the General Home Mission Committee shall be appointed as heretofore by the Synod, but that each District Board shall elect its own chairman, vice-chairman, secretary, and treasurer, for local purposes.

6. That the duty of the General Home Mission Committee shall be generally to watch over the interests of the Church as a whole in the department of Home Mission Work; and for this purpose the Committee shall meet in March, July, and November, with the other synodical committees—

(a) To receive reports from the District Boards;
(b) To call attention, when necessary, to any serious divergence of practice on the part of any District Board;
(c) To receive and dispose of appeals that may be taken against any decision of the District Board by a minority of the same after dissent duly taken;
(d) To make suggestions as to the initiation of new enterprises in the districts which District Boards may have overlooked;
(e) To consider suggestions and information given by the District Boards as to the policy to be followed

in Home Mission and Church Extension Work in the Church at large ; and—

(*f*) To allocate to the District Boards legacies not specially designated, and any other funds accruing for general Home Mission objects.

7. The General Committee shall also make the necessary arrangements for the visitation of Presbyteries by the Synod Deputies, as this may be from time to time appointed by the Synod, and also for the presentation of their reports, the expense of the visitation being chargeable on the funds of the districts within which respectively the visitation is made.

8. That each District Board shall initiate and superintend Home Mission, Church Extension, Church Building, and Evangelistic Work, in co-operation with the Presbyteries of the bounds, and shall raise and administer funds for these objects within its own district, under rules to be approved by the Synod, it being understood that the relation of the Presbyteries to the District Board shall be similar to, and stand in lieu of, that now existing between the Presbytery and the Home Mission Committee. Further, that each District Board shall receive from the several Presbyteries within its bounds reports in regard to the Evangelistic Work done throughout the year.

9. That each Local Treasurer shall send the funds raised by the District Board to the Financial Secretary of the Church, who shall keep a distinct account for each district. Congregational contributions to be remitted direct to the Church Offices as heretofore. The Treasurership Committee to distribute the funds on the order of the several District Boards, and to assign to each its share of the general expenses.

10. That District Boards shall submit their minutes at each meeting of the General Committee, together with a report of their work since the previous meeting ; and shall also submit to the March meeting a general report of their work throughout the year, together with a digest of the reports of the various Presbyteries in regard to Evangelistic Work done within their respective bounds.

11. That the General Home Mission Committee shall present one report to the Synod, including the substance of the annual reports of the several District Boards.

II.—RULES FOR THE ADMINISTRATION OF THE FUNDS.

A.—General Fund.

1. *Department of Church Extension.*

12. That the concurrence of the District Board be required before a Presbytery opens any new Station requiring aid, or takes any step towards its erection into a regular charge.

13. That applications for aid be made to the District Board, by means of schedules so constructed that the answers to the questions put shall furnish in each case full information in regard to the nature, position, and prospects of the enterprise for which assistance is sought, together with an extract Minute of the Presbytery within whose bounds the Congregation is situated, stating that the case has been carefully inquired into, and that the application is, in the judgment of the Presbytery, in all respects one which the Board ought to entertain; further, that all schedules be required to be in the hands of the Local Secretary at least a fortnight before the meeting of the Board.

14. That such schedules shall each contain a question as to the period within which the Congregation is likely to become self-supporting, and that assistance be ordinarily given from the Home Mission Fund only in cases in which the answer to that question is perfectly satisfactory.

15. That while, for the convenience of any Congregation prepared to call a Minister, the District Board may indicate a maximum scale of grants to be contemplated so far as necessary in any particular case, extending over a short term of years, dating from the settlement of the Minister, the Board shall not be held bound for the continuance of the grant, or for any specific amount in any given year, apart from due consideration of the position and requirements of the particular Congregation year by year, as shown in their statement of accounts and otherwise.

16. That every aided Congregation shall be required to furnish the District Board with an annual statement of accounts in the beginning of each year, duly attested by the Presbytery of the bounds.

2. *Department of Evangelistic Work.*

17. That financial assistance shall be furnished in the following cases, viz.:—

(a) In aid of regular Congregations situated in poor and densely peopled districts, and doing effective Evangelistic Work; such cases, however, to be taken up with great deliberation, and, if possible, in connection with strong Congregations capable of giving substantial help: the grant not to exceed £50 per annum.

(b) In aid of preaching stations under regular Presbyterial supervision but not likely to develop rapidly or at all into regular Congregations: the grant in no case to exceed £40 per annum.

(c) In aid of Congregational Mission Work designed, and in the judgment of the Presbytery so organized as to be likely, to grow into self-supporting and aggressive Congregations, grants may be made not exceeding one-third of the total cost, nor £75 in all in any one year. After three years of such grant the whole circumstances shall be again taken into consideration; and if it shall prove that further assistance is still needed, and in the judgment of the Board called for and desirable, the amount of the annual grant shall be continued, but gradually reduced so as to terminate within a further period of three years.

(d) In aid of a Congregation employing a Student or Probationer in systematic Evangelistic Work: the grant not to exceed £20 in amount, nor half the total salary paid.

(e) In connection with Special Evangelistic Services:—

(1) To individual Congregations—half the expense incurred being allowed where assistance is deemed necessary, and the amount sought reasonable; it being required, however, that when the sum to be asked from the Home Mission Fund is likely to exceed £5, the Presbytery of the bounds shall be consulted before the movement is initiated.

(2) In the case of organized effort by Presbyteries the Home Mission Boards shall be authorized to pay to the Treasurer of the Presbyterial Evangelisation Committee an amount equivalent to that which might have been claimed by the individual Congregations co-operating, had they been acting independently. Presbyteries shall in each case submit their whole scheme, and have the approval of their respective Boards, before any expense is incurred; and shall also be required to provide, through their respective Evangelisation Committees or otherwise, at least half the total expense incurred.

18. That all applications, whether for new grants or for the renewal of such as have previously been enjoyed, shall be made annually by means of schedules, with Presbyterial attestation and recommendation after full enquiry, and containing specific information in regard to the character and results of the Evangelistic Work on the ground of which the application is made; such schedules to be in the hands of the Local Secretary at least a fortnight before the meeting of the District Board.

19. That a statement of accounts, duly attested by the Presbytery of the bounds, shall be furnished in the beginning of each year to the District Board by all preaching stations and Congregations receiving grants under sub-sections 17 (*a*) and 17 (*b*).

20. That while, for the convenience of any Congregation desiring to initiate Home Mission Work under sub-section (*c*), the District Board may indicate a scale of grants contemplated and extending over a period of years not exceeding three, dating from the commencement of such work, the Board shall not be held responsible for the continuance of the grant, or for any specific amount in any given year, apart from the due consideration of the position and requirements of the particular effort year by year, as shown in the statement of accounts and otherwise.

B.—CHURCH BUILDING AND DEBT EXTINCTION FUND.

21. That the following general rules (paragraphs 22–34) shall apply to all Church Building enterprises aided from this fund:—

22. That the specific points which shall principally be considered in making grants be the following, viz.: sufficiency of accommodation (including separate and well-arranged provision for Sunday Schools), substantial construction and appropriate appearance of the building, adequate acoustics and ventilation, moderate cost, liberality of promoters, eligibility of site, satisfactory tenure, extent of population, deficiency of other evangelical provision.

23. That applications be made by means of schedules furnished by the District Board, and accompanied in each case with an extract minute of the Presbytery within whose bounds the Congregation is situated, stating that the application has been carefully inquired into, and is, in the judgment of the Presbytery, in all respects one which the Board ought to entertain. Further, that such schedules must be in the hands of the Local Secretary at least a fortnight before the meeting of the Board.

24. That there be also submitted to the District Board for their approval—

    (a) The plan of the proposed site, drawn on a scale of 16 feet to 1 inch, showing any surrounding buildings that may affect the lighting or ventilation of the intended Church.

    (b) The ground plan, gallery plan, front and side elevations, and one longitudinal and two transverse sections of the intended Church, Lecture-hall, Class-rooms, Session-house, and Minister's Vestry, all on a scale of 8 feet to 1 inch, and having all dimensions duly marked.

25. N.B.—Congregations proposing to erect Churches for which aid will be asked from the public funds are required to take counsel with the District Board at the very outset (before committing themselves to any architect or scheme) in regard to methods of procedure.

26. That no Church be eligible for pecuniary aid if the contract has been signed and the works commenced prior to such examination and approval of drawings by the District Board.

27. That the estimated cost must include boundary walls, lighting, heating, ventilation, and all fees (to solicitor, architect, surveyor, or others), so as to embrace the total amount of the ultimate outlay.

28. That no grant shall be regarded as finally made till there shall have been submitted to the District Board an approved tender with copy of the specifications and contract, showing that the works will be completed within the estimated cost, and a copy of the plans, specification, and contract as accepted shall be supplied to the District Board.

29. That grants may be made in suitable cases towards the purchase of Churches, provided the conditions prescribed in paragraph 22 are fully met.

30. That every grant made shall be on the distinct understanding that no mortgage shall be taken on the site, Church or Lecture-hall; and that should such a step at any subsequent time seem necessary, the sanction of the Presbytery and District Board must first be obtained, which shall only be given on condition of the repayment of so much of the grant as shall have been already paid.

31. That a trust deed be prepared and signed in accordance with the Synod's model deed, and submitted to the District Board for approval prior to the payment of the first portion of the grant.

32. That in case of any important departure, without the previous consent of the District Board, from the plans

and specifications approved by it, or in the event of the violation of these rules, the grant shall be forfeited.

33. That all future grants (April 26th, 1887) shall be subject to the following limits in regard to time, viz. :—

(1) That the grant shall lapse entirely—
(a) If the works shall not be commenced within one year from the date at which a grant is voted.
(b) If the Congregation shall not have found themselves able within two years to qualify for at least the first moiety.

(2) That all claim to any further payment shall cease if the Congregation shall not have qualified for the second payment within five years of the making of the grant.

(3) That all claims shall cease at the end of eight years.

(4) That, nevertheless, any portion or the whole of the grant may be renewed on fresh application.

34. That it be understood that the receivers of a grant for a Church shall abstain from personal application to subscribers to this fund residing beyond the bounds of the district within which said Church is situated, a list of such subscribers being furnished, if desired, by the General Committee.

35. That aid shall be given in two general classes of cases—

Class A. Church extension enterprises.

Class B. Congregations of older standing in which aid is needed in the necessary rebuilding of Churches, in the reconstruction or improvement of the Church property, or in the extinction of debt on the same.

36. That the following rules (paragraphs 37–45) shall regulate the grants of the District Boards in these two classes of cases respectively :—

Class A.

37. That the District Board shall make grants on the basis of a fifth of the entire cost (exclusive of site), the total grant in no case to exceed £1,400.

38. That no grant shall be made where the entire cost of the Church, Lecture-hall, Class-rooms, and Minister's Vestry (exclusive of site) shall exceed £7,000, unless in cases where there are more than 700 sittings provided.

39. That the grants made by the District Boards be paid as follows, viz. :—One-half when half of the entire estimated cost, including site and every probable outlay (less the grant), shall have been actually received by the

Congregational Treasurer; another quarter when three-fourths of the estimated cost (less the grant) shall have been so received; and the remaining quarter when seven-eighths of the entire actual cost (less the grant) shall have been so received.

40. N.B.—It will not be sufficient that the amount required shall have been *subscribed*, but it must have been actually *received*, and a certificate to that effect furnished to the District Board, along with a statement of the exact position of the Church Building Account.

Class B.

41. That the *maximum* grant be £250 in gift, with, in special cases, a *loan*, which, however, shall in no case exceed £250.

42. That in such cases the grant (whether of loan or gift, or both) shall bear proportion, on the one hand, to the cost of the building, and, on the other, to the amount likely to accrue from the sale of the former building (if any).

43. That payment of grants shall be arranged so as to secure that the Congregations aided are raising satisfactorily their own proportion of the amount needed; that no money shall in any case be advanced, either in gift or loan, till the building shall have been completed; and that a loan shall in no case be made payable till at least three-fourths of the actual cost of the Church and connected buildings shall have been otherwise raised, and a certificate to that effect, together with a full statement of account, furnished to the Committee.

44. That no grant shall be made for the re-building of a Church where the title-deeds are not satisfactory, or where the entire cost of the Church and connected buildings (exclusive of site) shall exceed £5,000, unless where there are more than 600 sittings, but that in such cases the cost must not exceed £8 per sitting.

45. That where loans are given without interest the following rules be strictly observed, viz.:—

> (a) That loans be advanced on personal security only, and repayable without interest in one or more sums as may be agreed upon, the general plan being for the loans to be returned in equal annual instalments not exceeding five.[1]

---

[1] The usual form of note is as follows:—
(Place.) (Date.)
One (or more) years after date we jointly and severally promise to pay A B C, or order   pounds for value received

(b) That if the loan be not applied for within one year of the date at which the grant is made, such grant shall lapse, but a renewed application may be made.

Class C.

46. That when a Presbytery proposes the erection of a new Church for working people in a densely populated district, which there is reasonable ground to expect may become self-supporting within seven years of its being opened, the Home Mission Committee be authorised and instructed to provide three-fourths of the cost of site and Church buildings, on condition that the Presbytery undertakes to provide the remaining fourth from within its own bounds.

47. The express sanction of the Synod shall be necessary in all such cases: and not more than one grant under this special rule shall be authorised by the Synod in any one year.

48. That, so far as applicable, the rules for Church building (pars. 22 to 40 inclusive) shall regulate the procedure under class C, it being specially noted that all such applications under this head are to be made to the Synod's Home Mission Committee through the District Boards.

F.—RULES FOR THE EMPLOYMENT OF LICENTIATES OR PROBATIONERS, AS AMENDED BY THE SYNOD IN 1881 AND 1890.

1. That correct Rolls be made up as follows, viz.:—

   Roll A—for the supply of vacant charges.
   Roll B—for occasional supply.
   Roll C—of vacant charges.
   Roll D—of preaching stations.

2. That in order to the preparation of said Rolls, Presbytery Clerks are instructed to notify to the General Secretary—

   (a) The licences to preach granted from time to time by Presbyteries, with dates of licence.
   (b) The names of ordained Ministers without

---

on loan from the Church Building Fund of the Presbyterian Church of England.

Payable at Bank } Signed

These notes must be written on stamped paper, and signed by from four to eight persons approved by the Board (deacons, managers, trustees, or others), the address of each signer to be added, and also the name and address of the Banker to whom the note, when due, may be presented for payment.

charges who seek to be placed on the Roll, with dates of ordination.

(c) The vacant charges and preaching stations, with names of *interim* Moderators of Sessions.

3. That names shall be placed on Roll A, according to the following regulations:—

(a) Licentiates, on the report of their licence to the Committee by the Clerk of the licensing Presbytery.

(b) Ordained Ministers resigning their charges, on the concurrent judgment of the Committee and their respective Presbyteries, that it is expedient that their names be placed on this Roll.

(c) Licentiates, and ordained Ministers without charges from other Churches, only on direct appointment of the Synod, except in the case of those coming from any of the other *Federated* Churches, whose names are placed on Roll A, on the concurrent approval of the Committee, and the several Presbyteries under whose care they may have placed themselves.

(d) That the right of Presbyteries, when receiving Ministers and Licentiates from the other Federated Churches, to make such enquiry regarding them as may appear necessary, owing to the form of their Presbyterial credentials not being satisfactory, or to other circumstances, is fully recognised.

4. That Probationers shall be entitled to appointments to vacant charges or preaching stations for a period of *six* years from the date of licence; and ordained Ministers without charge to an equal privilege in respect of appointments to vacancies or preaching stations, for a period of *three* years from the date of their being received on the Roll: it being understood—

(a) That when any one has been laid aside by lengthened sickness, the time so consumed shall not be included in the term of probation.

(b) That in the case of Probationers and Ministers who have been received from other Churches, the time they may have spent on the Probationers' Roll of said Churches shall be counted as part of the term allowed by this Church; no departure from this rule to be allowed in any case without the permission of the Synod.

5. Roll B shall consist of Licentiates and ordained Ministers who are not on Roll A, and are willing to render occasional pulpit service; such names to be placed on this Roll (as on Roll A), on the concurrent judgment of the Committee and their respective Presbyteries, that it is expedient to do so.

6. That vacant congregations be supplied by this Committee from the Probationers on Roll A; and that vacant Congregations who wish to keep arrangements for supply in their own hands, be instructed to notify the same to the General Secretary, and be recommended to employ Probationers on the Roll as far as possible: it being understood—

> That vacant Congregations shall not make arrangements for supply with any one on the Roll, nor any one on the Roll make application to be heard in vacant Congregations, except through the Committee.

7. That when a Session or Congregation desire the services of a particular Probationer or Minister, they shall communicate that desire, through the Clerk of Presbytery or Moderator of Session, to the General Secretary, who shall give effect to it as soon as practicable, on the condition that any expenses or losses incurred by displacements (if any) thereby made in the list of appointments shall be borne by the Congregation at whose request the change is made.

8. That appointments to vacant Congregations do not exceed two Sabbaths at one time, or to preaching stations, three months, unless by special arrangements made by the Presbytery through the Committee.

9. That the Committee meet in March, July, and November, to superintend the work, but that applications for supply and the arrangement of appointments to Congregations and stations shall be entrusted meanwhile to the General Secretary of the Church.

10. That when a Probationer accepts a Call, he shall give notice to the General Secretary. No further appointments to vacant Congregations shall be made to him, and any appointments of this nature in his hand at the time shall be cancelled.

11. The following scale is recommended as a fair remuneration to Probationers for their services in vacant Congregations and preaching stations, viz.:—

    (*a*) £1 1*s.* per Sabbath where the contribution of the Congregation towards stipend is £150 and under.

    (*b*) £1 10*s.* per Sabbath where the contribution of the Congregation towards stipend is above £150 and not more than £200.

    (*c*) £2 2*s.* per Sabbath where the stipend is above £200.

These fees are exclusive of board, and of travelling expenses one way.

G.—THE THEOLOGICAL COLLEGE.

This College was established in the year 1844 by the Synod of the Presbyterian Church in England for the purpose of affording Theological instruction to Students for the Ministry of that Church.

CONSTITUTION OF THE SENATUS.

I.—The Senatus is composed of the Principal and the Professors; the Principal presiding at its meetings, or in his absence, the Senior Professor.

II.—The Senatus arranges and determines what classes the students attend in the different years of their studies; and the hours of their attendance.

III.—The Senatus decides on the exercises rendered, and the discourses delivered by the students during their attendance at College, as to whether they are to be sustained, and to form part of the course required by the Church.

IV.—The Senatus pronounces judgment in every case in which the laws of the College have been infringed, with power to call in the Visitors (appointed by the Synod in connection with College matters) in such instances as to its wisdom seems fit.

V.—The Senatus, in conjunction with the Library Committee, regulates the use of the Library by the students and others, subject to such rules as the Synod may lay down or approve.

VI.—The Senatus makes an annual report to the Synod of the work done in the previous Session.

BOARD OF EXAMINATION.

The constitution of the Board was determined by the Synod of 1883, as follows:—

I.—That the Board consist of eight examining members, besides the official members and a Chairman and Secretary.

II.—That one of these eight retire each year.

III.—That retiring members be open to re-election after an interval of two years.

IV.—That the Synod shall appoint members to fill up vacancies on the Board on the recommendation of the Board itself.

V.—That the members of the Board shall be ex-officio members of the College Committee, without prejudice to the number provided for by the rules of the Church.

COURSE OF STUDY.

The course of study extends over three years, the term of study in each year commencing in the first week of October and ending in the last week of April.

The Classes, which are distributed over three years of attendance, embrace the following subjects of study:—

> Dogmatics.
> History of Doctrine.
> Practical Theology.
>
> New Testament Exegesis and Criticism.
> Church History.
>
> Old Testament Exegesis and Criticism.
> Apologetics.

REGULATIONS FOR THE ADMISSION OF STUDENTS.

I.—In all cases a certificate of Church membership and a pastoral testimonial are indispensable to admission, and likewise a medical certificate, satisfactory to the Board, of fitness to engage in a course of study with a view to the Ministry.

II.—In the case of applicants who are members of the Presbyterian Church of England, they are likewise required to produce to the Board a certificate from the Presbytery within the bounds of which they reside, that they have satisfied the Presbytery respecting their motives, religious character, and probable usefulness in the Ministry. Intending Students are requested to send in their names to the Clerk of their Presbytery not later than the first day of July.

III.—No Student shall be entered on the roll of the College as a regular Theological Student of the First Year unless he shall produce either—

a A diploma of M.A. or B.A. from a chartered University of the British Empire; or,

b Class tickets and certificates of attendance at a College or University for three Sessions, and a certificate from the Synod's Board of Examination, that he has satisfactorily passed an examination, conducted by Printed Papers and Orally, in the English Bible, History, Latin, Greek, Mathematics, Mental and Moral Philosophy (including Logic), and in one or other of the following subjects, at his option; viz. (*a*) A branch of Physical or Natural Science; (*b*) English History and Literature; or (*c*) one of the Modern Languages.

IV.—All candidates for entrance, graduates included, are required to pass an examination in Elementary Hebrew, on Sections 1–30 of Dr. A. B. Davidson's Introductory Hebrew Grammar, and to write an Essay on some popular subject, to be announced in the room on the day of examination.

V.—No Student of another Church who contemplates the office of the Ministry in this Church shall be entered on the roll of the College as a regular Theological Student of the Second or Third Year, unless he shall produce, in addition to his theological certificates, either—

    (1) As above (III., *a*); or,
    (2) A certificate that he has successfully passed the Examination Board of a sister Presbyterian Church; or,
    (3) A certificate from the Synod's Board of Examination that he has satisfactorily passed an examination, conducted by Printed Papers and Orally, in the subjects named above (III., *b*), with the addition of Hebrew and Theology; and further that he has satisfied the Board respecting his motives, religious character, and probable usefulness in the Ministry.

VI.—Students who have not complied with the foregoing regulation (III., *b*) must apply to the Board of Examination, who shall inquire into and judge of the sufficiency of the reasons assigned for seeking admission, and report to the College Committee; should these reasons appear satisfactory, the College Committee shall have power to admit the applicant at once to the Board Examination. This Regulation applies only to members of the Presbyterian Church of England.

Rules as to attendance at the Theological Colleges of the Free Church of Scotland and the Theological College of the Presbyterian Church of England.

The following Extract from an Act of the General Assembly of the Free Church in 1888, which was concurred in by the Synod of the Presbyterian Church of England in 1889, has the force of law in the cases to which it refers:—

"The Assembly hereby approve of the provisional suggestions submitted by the College Committee in Appendix III. of the Report, and enact said Regulations as the Regulations under which attendance at the Hall of the Presbyterian Church of England shall be recognised by the Colleges and Presbyteries of this Church, as equivalent to corresponding attendance at one of the Free Church Colleges, as follows:—

"'No Student or probationer from either Church shall be entitled to claim the benefit of reception in the other, on the footing of equality, in whose case the following conditions have not been complied with:—

"'(*a*) ENTRANCE TO HALL.—Students must have entered either (1) as Graduates in Arts of a known teaching University, with a curriculum of not less than three years, or of the University of London; or (2) as having studied a full Undergraduate Course of not less than three years, at a known teaching University, and successfully passed the Entrance Examination of their Church—*i.e.*, of the Church in which they are certified members.

"'(*b*) PASSAGE FROM ENGLISH PRESBYTERIAN TO FREE CHURCH HALLS (and *vice versâ*) IN THE CASE OF STUDENTS GOING THROUGH THEIR THEOLOGICAL COURSE.—Students who divide their studies between the Hall of the English Presbyterian Church and the Halls of the Free Church must complete four sessions.

"'(*c*) EXIT.—Students must successfully pass the Exit Examination of a Church in whose Hall or Halls they have studied for two years at least."

"'Therefore, students in whose case the full examination, either Entrance or Exit, has been dispensed with, either by the English Presbyterian College Committee, or by the Free Church Assembly, shall not be entitled under the Act to claim equality of standing as students or probationers.'"

REGULATIONS FOR EXAMINATIONS.

All Students seeking admission to the classes of the First, Second, or Third Year are examined, by Printed Papers, on books and subjects previously announced. The Examinations are held in the first week of October. Students who pass the Examinations with Honours are entitled to have their names published in an Honour List. Scholarships are awarded to the Students who gain the highest number of marks with Honours in the order of their numbers.

All Students, at the close of their course of study in the College, are required to pass the Exit Examination, by Printed Papers, on books and subjects previously prescribed and made known. Certificates of their having passed this Examination are requisite to their being taken on trial for license as Preachers of the Gospel by the Presbyteries of the Church.

The Board conduct all the Examinations for Entrance of Students in their respective years, for Scholarships, and for Exit. They grant certificates of Pass and of Honours for Entrance and for Exit, and they award all Scholarships connected with the College.

Inquiries and applications regarding Examinations and the Scholarships attached to the College, Undergraduate and Theological, should be addressed to the Rev. William Ballantyne, 31, Clissold Road, Stoke Newington, London, N.; for Undergraduate Scholarships, not later than 1st of August, and for Entrance and Theological Scholarships, not later than 1st of September.

CLASS AND LIBRARY FEES.

All Students pay a fee of £5 5s. per Session for Classes and the use of the Library.

RESIDENCE.

A limited number of rooms (not more than fifteen) are provided in College for students who desire to be in residence. Students in residence pay an additional sum of £7 10s. per session for their rooms. The expense of Boarding is left for arrangement between the Resident Students and the House-Steward.

Inquiries regarding the College, Studies, Residence, and other arrangements should be addressed to the Rev. Professor Gibb, D.D., Queen Square House, Guilford Street, London, W.C.

SCHOLARSHIPS.

A.—*Undergraduate.*

The following Scholarships are open for competition by Students preparing for the Ministry of the Presbyterian Church of England, either entering upon or prosecuting their Undergraduate Course in a Chartered University or in a College affiliated therewith:—

1. The Robertson Scholarship: value £30 per annum, tenable for three years.
2. The Hamilton Scholarship: value £40 per annum, tenable for three years.
3. The Duncan Scholarship: value £25 per annum, tenable for three years.
4. The Anderson Scholarship: value £20 per annum, tenable for three years.
5. The McKerrow Scholarship: value £20 per annum, tenable for two years at Owen's College, Manchester.

B.—*Theological.*

1. The Gillespie Scholarship: value £50 per annum, tenable for three years. Open only to Students of the second year; the third year of tenure to be passed at an approved University on the Continent.
2. The Crichton Scholarship: value £25 per annum.
3. Newcastle Scholarship: value £25.
4. Muter Scholarships: Three of value £30 each; the holders must be abstainers from tobacco and alcoholic liquors.

5. Munro Scholarship: value £25 per annum.

6. Trail Scholarship: value £25 per annum, tenable for one year, the power of election being vested in the Senatus.

RECONSTRUCTION OF SCHOLARSHIPS.

A scheme of reconstruction of Theological Scholarships, promoted by the late Dr. Elmslie, was adopted by the Synod of 1889, and is gradually attaining completion. Its object is to provide four Scholarships of the minimum value of £50, one for each year of study, and the fourth a Travelling Fellowship, to be awarded to the student standing highest in the Exit Examination.

I. First Year.—Munro and Trail combined.
II. Second Year.—Gillespie, or Crichton and Newcastle combined.
III. Third Year.—Crichton and Newcastle; or Gillespie (without competition*), or Barbour Scholarship.

BARBOUR RESIDENTIAL EXHIBITIONS.

A sum of £5,000 was bequeathed to the College by a munificent benefactor of the Presbyterian Church, the late Robert Barbour, Esq., of Bolesworth, who died in 1885. The design of the bequest was "to provide Bursaries or Exhibitions or Scholarships to aid and encourage young men in attending the Presbyterian College."

In 1887 the Synod resolved to employ the income from this legacy in granting non-competitive Residential Exhibitions to suitable regular students of the Church, and constituted a Board for the administration of the Fund, consisting of the Principal and Professors, the Convener and Secretary of the College Committee, and the Convener and Secretary of the Board of Examination.

The Barbour Board is also authorised "in any year in which the Gillespie Scholarship is held as a Travelling Fellowship, to put at the disposal of the Board of Examination a sum not exceeding £50 towards a Barbour competitive Scholarship; (2) in other years, provided their funds appear to them to permit of it, to put at the disposal of the Board of Examination a sum not exceeding £50 towards a Travelling Fellowship, to be awarded to the student standing highest in the Exit Examination."

---

* With the exception of the Gillespie, whose tenure is fixed by deed, all these Scholarships are assigned for one year only, to the Student standing highest in the Entrance Examination of each year.

The Muter Scholarships of £30 each continue as before to serve as second prizes in each year.

Exhibitions vary in value up to £20, and are tenable for one year. The Board in granting them take into consideration the Scholarships and other Exhibitions held by the Students applying, and their ascertained requirements. Students residing in the College have a preferential claim.

Inquiries and applications regarding these Exhibitions should be addressed to Mr. J. G. Smieton, M.A., Secretary to the Barbour Board, Queen Square House, Guilford Street, London, W.C.

OUTSIDE SCHOLARSHIPS.

The following Exhibitions and Scholarships, although not belonging to this College, are open to be held by students of the Presbyterian Church of England.

(1) Hewley Exhibitions.

Five or six Hewley Exhibitions, value £40 per annum, are annually adjudged to students of this College, at the option of the Hewley Trustees, to whom application has to be made.

Communications respecting these Exhibitions should be addressed to Samuel Stitt, Esq., The Grange, Claughton, Birkenhead.

(2) Dr. Williams Scholarships.

Scholarships, both Undergraduate and Theological, known as the "Dr. Williams" Scholarships, value £40 and £50 respectively per annum, are annually awarded, by competition, under conditions which allow of their being held by students intending the ministry of the Presbyterian Church of England. Inquiries respecting these Scholarships should be addressed to the Secretary, Dr. Williams' Library, Gordon Square, London, W.C.

H.—FORMULAS.

I.—For Use at the Ordination or Induction of a Minister.

1. Do you believe the Scriptures of the Old and New Testaments to be the Word of God, and the only Rule of Faith and Duty?

2. Do you sincerely own and believe, as in accordance with Holy Scripture, and will you faithfully teach, the body of Christian doctrine set forth in the Westminster Confession of Faith and the other Subordinate Standards

of this Church, and now more briefly expressed in the XXIV. "Articles of the Faith" approved by the Synod of 1890?

3. Do you acknowledge the Appendix to the Articles of the Faith as expressing the general opinion and belief entertained in this Church on the matters to which it refers; and do you engage to regulate your action as a Minister of this Church in accordance with that Document?

4. Are you persuaded that the Lord Jesus Christ, the only King and Head of the Church, has therein appointed a government distinct from, and not subordinate to, civil government; and that, while rulers are bound to render obedience to Christ in their own province, yet they ought not to attempt in any way to constrain men's religious belief or invade the rights of conscience; and do you acknowledge the Presbyterian form of government to be founded on, and agreeable to, the Word of God?

5. Do you promise, as a Minister of this Church, to be subject to its government, and to take due part in the administration of its affairs; and, while cherishing brotherly love towards all the faithful followers of Christ, do you engage to seek the purity, peace, and extension of this Church?

6. Are zeal for the glory of God, love to the Lord Jesus Christ, and a desire to save souls, and not worldly designs or interests, as far as you know your own heart, your great motives and chief inducements to enter into the Office of the Holy Ministry?

[In case of Induction, after the word "enter," read "in this place on the discharge of the functions of your Sacred Office?"]

*7. Do you engage in the strength and grace of Jesus Christ, our Lord and Master, to live a holy and circumspect life, and faithfully to discharge all the parts of the ministerial work among this people, to the edifying of

---

* NOTES ON USE OF FORMULA I.

A.—*Special Question for Use at Induction of Professors of Theology, instead of No. 7.*

Do you engage, in the strength and grace of Jesus Christ, our Lord and Master, to live a holy and circumspect life, and faithfully to discharge all the parts of the work assigned to you as Professor of Theology [or, *of Church History, specially designating the Professorship*] in the Theological College of this Church, to the training of the Students under your care for the office of the Holy Ministry of the Gospel, and the edifying of the body of Christ, and to be zealous in maintaining the truth of the Gospel, whatever trouble or persecution may arise?

B.—*Special Question for Use at Ordination of Missionaries, instead of No. 7.*

Do you engage, in the strength and grace of Jesus Christ, our

the body of Christ, and to be zealous in maintaining the truth of the Gospel, whatever trouble or persecution may arise?

8. And all these things you profess and promise through grace, as you shall be answerable at the coming of the Lord Jesus, with all His saints, and as you would be accepted of Him, at His glorious appearing?

II.—For Use at the Licensing of Preachers.

1. Do you believe the Scriptures of the Old and New Testaments to be the Word of God and the only Rule of Faith and Duty?

2. Do you sincerely own and believe, as in accordance with Holy Scripture, and will you faithfully teach the body of Christian doctrine set forth in the Westminster Confession of Faith and the other Subordinate Standards of this Church, and now more briefly expressed in the XXIV. "Articles of the Faith" approved by the Synod of 1890?

3. Do you acknowledge the Appendix to the Articles of the Faith as expressing the general opinion and belief entertained in this Church on the matters to which it refers; and do you engage to regulate your action as a Probationer of this Church in accordance with that Document?

4. Are you persuaded that the Lord Jesus Christ, the only King and Head of the Church, has therein appointed a government distinct from, and not subordinate to, civil government; and that, while rulers are bound to render obedience to Christ in their own province, yet they ought not to attempt in any way to constrain men's religious belief or invade the rights of conscience; and do you acknowledge the Presbyterian form of government to be founded on, and agreeable to, the Word of God?

5. Do you promise as a Probationer for the Ministry of this Church, to be subject to its government, and, while cherishing brotherly love to all the faithful followers of Christ, do you engage to seek the purity, peace, and extension of this Church?

Lord and Master, to live a holy and circumspect life, and faithfully to discharge all the parts of the Ministerial work in the fulfilment of the duties of your office as a Missionary to China [or India, specially designating the field of labour] to the propagating of the Gospel among the people to whom you are sent forth, and the edifying of the body of Christ, and to be zealous in maintaining the truth of the Gospel, whatever trouble or persecution may arise?

C.—*At the Admission of a Minister from another Church, omit Question No. 7.*

6. Are zeal for the glory of God, love to the Lord Jesus Christ, and a desire to save souls, and not worldly designs or interests, so far as you know your own heart, your great motives and chief inducements for desiring to enter into the office of the Holy Ministry?

7. Do you engage in the strength and grace of Jesus Christ, our Lord and Master, to live a holy and circumspect life, and faithfully to discharge all the parts of the work of a Probationer for the office of the Holy Ministry?

8. And all these things you profess and promise through grace, as you shall be answerable at the coming of the Lord Jesus Christ with all His saints, and as you would be accepted of Him at His glorious appearing?

III.—For Use at the Ordination or Induction of Elders.

1. Do you believe the Scriptures of the Old and New Testaments to be the Word of God, and the only Rule of Faith and Duty?

2. Do you sincerely own and believe, as in accordance with Holy Scripture, the body of Christian doctrine set forth in the Westminster Confession of Faith and the other subordinate Standards of this Church, and now more briefly expressed in the XXIV. "Articles of the Faith," approved by the Synod of 1890?

3. Do you acknowledge the Appendix to the Articles of the Faith as expressing the general opinion and belief entertained in this Church on the matters to which it refers; and do you engage to regulate your action as an Elder of this Church in accordance with that Document?

4. Are you persuaded that the Lord Jesus Christ, the only King and Head of the Church, has therein appointed a government distinct from, and not subordinate to, civil government; and that, while rulers are bound to render obedience to Christ in their own province, yet they ought not in any way to constrain men's religious belief or invade the rights of conscience; and do you acknowledge the Presbyterian form of government to be founded on, and agreeable to, the Word of God?

5. Do you promise, as an Elder of this Church, to be subject to its government, and to take due part in the administration of its affairs; and while cherishing brotherly love towards all the faithful followers of Christ, do you engage to seek the purity, peace, and extension of this Church?

6. Do you engage in the strength and grace of Jesus Christ, our Lord and Master, to live a holy and circumspect life, to rule well your own house; and faithfully to

discharge the duties of the Eldership among this people to the edifying of the body of Christ?

7. And all these things you profess and promise through grace, as you shall be answerable at the coming of our Lord Jesus Christ, and as you would be accepted of Him at His glorious appearing?

IV.—For Use at the Ordination or Induction of Deacons.

1. Do you believe the Scriptures of the Old and New Testaments to be the Word of God, and the only Rule of Faith and Duty?

2. Do you sincerely receive and adopt, as in accordance with Holy Scripture, the system of Evangelical Doctrine held by this Church?

3. Do you engage in the strength and grace of Jesus Christ, our Lord and Master, to rule well your own house, and faithfully to discharge the duties of the Deacon's office among this people?

I.—CALLS.

I.— Form of Call to a Vacant Pastorate.

We, the undersigned Office-Bearers, and other Members of the Presbyterian Congregation of   , desirous of promoting the glory of God and the good of the Church, being without a fixed pastor, and being assured by good information or our own experience of the piety, prudence, and other ministerial qualifications of you   Preacher (or Minister) of the Gospel, have agreed to invite and call, as we do by these presents, heartily invite and call you to undertake the office of Pastor among us; and further, upon your accepting this our Call, and being inducted into the pastoral care of this Congregation, promise you all dutiful respect, encouragement, support, and obedience in the Lord.

In witness whereof we have hereunto subscribed with our hands this   day of   , one thousand eight hundred and   years.

II.—Form of Call to a Collegiate Pastorate.

We, the undersigned Office-Bearers, and other Members of the Presbyterian Congregation of   , desirous of promoting the glory of God and the good

of the Church, considering the desirableness of having a Colleague and Successor now appointed to the Rev.   , our present Pastor, and being assured by good information or our own experience of the piety, prudence, and other ministerial qualifications of you   Preacher (or Minister) of the Gospel, have agreed to invite and call, as we do by these presents heartily invite and call you to undertake the office of Colleague and Successor to the said Rev.
our Pastor; and further, upon your accepting this our Call and being inducted, promise you all dutiful respect, encouragement, and obedience in the Lord.

In witness whereof we have hereunto subscribed with our hands this   day of   , one thousand eight hundred and   years.

III.—Form of Concurrence in Call to a Minister.

We, the undersigned, usually worshipping in   Presbyterian Church,   , hereby signify our hearty concurrence with the members thereof in the Call which they have addressed to   to become their Pastor. [In the case of a Colleague and Successor, add the words, "As Colleague and Successor to the Rev.   ."]

IV.—Form of Attestation of Call by the Minister appointed to preside at the giving of a Call.

The above names, to the number of   , were subscribed in my presence, this   day of   , 18   .

            , Minister.

V.—Form of Attestation of Call by the Moderator of Presbytery at the giving of a Call.

The above names, to the number of   , were subscribed in the presence of the Presbytery of   this   day of   , 18   .

            , Moderator.

VI.—Form of Attestation of Call by Members of Session.

The above names, to the number of   , were subscribed in our presence, this   day of   , 18

            , Elder.
            , Elder.

J.—EDICTS.

Edicts are read from the pulpit in the hearing of the Congregation, and are certified, for the Presbytery, in such terms as the following:—

The above Edict was read by me in the presence of the Congregation, this   day of   , 18 .
                                        , *Officiating Minister.*
  (Witness)
  (Witness)

I.—Of Vacancy in a Pastoral Charge.

It is hereby intimated, in name and by appointment of the Presbytery of   , that the pastoral charge of this Church is now vacant in consequence of [*here state the cause of the vacancy, such as the death, or the resignation*] of   , the late Minister thereof; and further, that the Office-bearers and Members of this Congregation are now called upon to take steps to fill up the said vacancy with all convenient speed, in accordance with the rules of the Presbyterian Church of England.

II.—Of the Call to a Minister.

1. It is hereby intimated, in the name and by the appointment of the Presbytery of   , that, in consequence of an application from the Session of this Congregation, the Presbytery appointed that the giving of a Call to a Minister to fill up the vacancy in the pastoral charge of this Congregation, take place within this Church, on   , the   day of   , 18 , at   o'clock: the Rev.   to preach and preside.

2. It is hereby intimated, in the name and by the appointment of the Presbytery of   , that, in consequence of an application from the Session, the Presbytery resolved to meet within this Church on   , the   day of   , 18 , at o'clock, at the giving of a Call to a Minister to fill up the vacancy in the pastoral charge of this Congregation: the Rev.   to preach and preside.

III.—Of Ordination or Induction of a Minister.

The Presbytery of   having resolved to proceed to the Ordination (or Induction) of A. B., who has been duly called to be Minister of this Congregation, hereby give notice to the Members of this Congregation,

that if any of them have anything to object to the character or teaching of the said A. B.   , they must appear before the Presbytery which is to meet in   , on   , the   day of   , 18   , at   o'clock ; and further, that if no relevant objection be then made and proved, the Presbytery will proceed to the Ordination (or, *in the case of an ordained Minister*, to the Induction) of the said A. B.   , and to his admission to the pastoral charge of this Congregation.
 Attested by
           , *Presbytery Clerk.*

IV.—OF ORDINATION OR INDUCTION OF ELDERS OR DEACONS.

 The Session of this Congregation having appointed an election of Elders to take place on the   day of   , 18   , and the Congregation, after due notice, having made choice of the following persons, namely :—   , and the Session having sustained the election, and the aforesaid brethren, having intimated their (*or* his) acceptance of the office, the Session did, on the   day of   , 18   , appoint the ordination and admission to the office of the Eldership of the said brethren [and, *if any person or persons chosen have been already ordained*, the induction of the said   ],   , to take place on   , the   day of   , 18   . It is accordingly hereby intimated that if any members of this Congregation have any objections to offer to the character or doctrinal opinions of the said A. B., etc., they must appear at a meeting of the Session, to be held in   , on   the   day of   , at   o'clock ; and further, that if no relevant objection be then made and proved, the Session will proceed to the ordination of the said   [and, *in the case of the person or persons already ordained*, the induction of the said   ], on   , the   day of   , 18   , at   o'clock.
 Attested by
           , *Session Clerk.*

V.—OF PROPOSED TRANSFERENCE OF A MINISTER.

 1. Having received official notice that a Call from the Congregation of   to the Rev. A. B., Minister of this Congregation, has been sustained by the Presbytery of   , I hereby cite the Session and Congregation of this Church to appear for their interests in connection with said Call at a meeting of the Presbytery of   , to be held in   on the   at   o'clock ; and further, give notice

that, if they do not appear, they will be held as consenting to the transference of the Rev. A. B. from
    to   .

           , *Presbytery Clerk.*

2. A Call from the   Church to the Rev. A. B, Minister of this Church, to be their Pastor, having been laid upon their table, the Presbytery of   , at their meeting upon the   day of   , resolved to make intimation thereof to this Congregation; and further, to cite the Session, and the Congregation of this Church, to appear for their interests at the next ordinary meeting of the Presbytery, to be held at   , on the   day of   next, at   o'clock; further, to give notice that if they do not appear, they will be held as consenting to the transference of the Rev. A. B. from
    to   .

VI.—Of the Resignation of a Minister.

The resignation of the Rev. A. B.   , of the Pastorate of this Church, having been laid upon their table, the Presbytery of   , at their meeting upon the   day of   , resolved to make intimation thereof to this Congregation; and further, to cite the Session and Congregation to appear for their interests at the meeting of the Presbytery, to be held at   , on the   day of   next, at   o'clock, that they may state their reasons, if they have any, why Mr.   's resignation should not proceed; and further, to give notice that if they do not appear, they will be held as consenting to such resignation.

VII.—Of Admission of Minister and Congregation from Another Communion.

Application for admission into the Presbyterian Church of England having been made by this Congregation, as also by the Pastor, to the Presbytery of   , and the Presbytery, after full inquiry and consideration, having applied to the Synod for permission to receive them; and this permission having been granted, the Presbytery, on the   day of   , resolved to meet in this place on the   day of   , at   o'clock, to receive and admit this Congregation and their Pastor into union with the Presbyterian Church of England.

K.—FORMS OF CERTIFICATES.

I.—Form of Certificate of Membership in Full Communion.

It is hereby certified that Mr. A. B. is a Member of the Congregation of   , and in full communion with the Presbyterian Church of England, and is commended to the fellowship of the Congregation into which he is now led to seek admission.

                                                , *Minister.*
                                                , *Session Clerk.*
           , Place.
           , Date.

II.— Form of Certificate of Eldership.

It is hereby certified, on the   day of 18 , in the name and by the authority of the Session of the Congregation of   , that Mr.   is an acting member thereof.

                                                , *Session Clerk.*

III.—Form of Certificate of Licence of Preacher.

It is hereby certified, in the name and by the authority of the Presbytery of   , that Mr.   having passed the curriculum of study prescribed by the rules of the Presbyterian Church of England; having passed the Exit Examination by the Synod's Board of Examination in Systematic and Practical Theology, Church History, Hebrew, Greek, and the Exegesis of the Old and New Testaments; and having presented Certificates of character and attainments, was taken on trials for Licence by the Presbytery of   ; that having passed such trials to the satisfaction of said Presbytery, and having given satisfactory answers to the questions prescribed to Candidates for Licence, he was on the   day of   , 18 , duly licensed to preach the Gospel within the bounds, and wheresoever he may be called in an orderly manner, as a Probationer for the office of the Holy Ministry.

                                                , *Presbytery Clerk.*

IV.—Form of Certificate to Preacher on Going from one Presbytery to Another.

That Mr.   , who is duly licensed by this Church to preach the Gospel, has resided within the bounds of this Presbytery for the past   ; [that

he has exercised his gifts as a preacher to the satisfaction of the members thereof who have had an opportunity of hearing him;] and that he has conducted himself, as far as known to them, in a way becoming his position as a Probationer for the office of the Holy Ministry; is certified at   , in name and by appointment of the Presbytery of   , this   day   , one thousand, eight hundred and   years, by
Presbytery Clerk.

V.—FORM OF CERTIFICATE TO ORDAINED MINISTER WITHOUT CHARGE ON GOING FROM ONE PRESBYTERY TO ANOTHER.

That the Rev.   , Minister of the Gospel, without pastoral charge, has resided within the bounds of this Presbytery for the past   ; that he has exercised his ministry in several of its Congregations as opportunity offered; and that his character and conduct, so far as known to the members, have been in all respects consistent with his position as a Christian Minister, is certified at   , in name and by authority of the Presbytery of   , this   day of   , one thousand eight hundred and   years, by
        , *Presbytery Clerk.*

VI.—CERTIFICATE OF TRANSFER OF A STUDENT IN THEOLOGY FROM ONE PRESBYTERY TO ANOTHER.

1. It is hereby certified that Mr.   , Student in Theology, of the [*first*] Year, hitherto under the care of the Presbytery of   , who are satisfied with his proficiency and character, is, at his own request, transferred to the care of the Presbytery of   , within whose bounds he goes to reside.
        , *Presbytery Clerk.*

2. It is hereby certified that Mr.   , Student in Theology, having completed the curriculum of study, and passed the Exit Examination prescribed by the rules of the Church, and having produced satisfactory evidence of his attainments and character, was duly taken on trials in order to his being duly licensed to preach the Gospel by the Presbytery of   ; that he had the following subjects of trials prescribed to him,
and that, being about to leave the bounds of this Presbytery, he requested to have his trials transferred to the Presbytery of   , within the bounds of which he is going to reside; that his request to that effect has been granted, and that he is recommended to the aforesaid Presbytery of   as a Student on public trials for Licence as a Probationer of the Church.
        , *Presbytery Clerk.*

L.—FORMS OF COMMISSIONS.

I.—Forms of Elder's Commission to the Presbytery.

1. It is hereby certified, in the name and by the authority of the Session of   Church, that, on the   day of   , 18   , Mr.   , one of the acting Members thereof, was duly appointed to represent them in the Presbytery of   , during the currency of the next   months.
, *Session Clerk.*

2. It is hereby certified, in the name and by the authority of the Session of   Church, that, on the   day of   , 18   , Mr.   , an acting Member of the Session of   , was duly appointed to represent the said Session of   , in the Presbytery of   during the currency of the next   months.
, *Session Clerk.*

It is hereby certified, on the   day of   , 18   , in the name and by the authority of the Session of the Congregation of   , that the aforesaid Mr.   is an Acting Member thereof.
, *Session Clerk.*

II.—Form of Elder's Commission to the Synod.

1. At   , the   day of   , 18   .

It is hereby certified, in the name and by the authority of the Session of   Presbyterian Church, that on the   day of   18   , Mr.   , Ruling Elder, was duly appointed to represent the said Session in the Synod of the Presbyterian Church of England at its Meeting appointed to be held at   , on   the   day of   , 18   .
, *Session Clerk.*

2. At   , the   day of   , 18

It is hereby certified, in the name and by the authority of the Session of   Presbyterian Church, that Mr.   is an acting Member thereof.
, *Session Clerk.*

Note.—Elders must have Certificate No. 2. from the Session of which they are Members, whether elected to represent their own or any other Session.

M.—FORMS OF NOTICES.

I.—Meetings of Congregation for Filling up of Vacancy in a Pastoral Charge.

1. Notice is hereby given that, by appointment of the Session, a meeting of this Congregation will be held in   , on   , the   day of   , at   o'clock, for the purpose of considering the steps to be taken for filling up the vacancy in the Pastoral Charge of this Congregation, in consequence of the [Resignation or otherwise] of the Rev.   , late Minister thereof; the Rev.   , Moderator of Session *ad interim*, to preside on this occasion.

Attested by
, *Session Clerk.*

2. Notice is hereby given that, by appointment of the Session, a meeting of this Congregation will be held in   , on   , the   day of   , at   o'clock, for the purpose of ascertaining whether the Congregation is ripe for the election of a Minister, and for application to the Presbytery to grant opportunity for giving a Call; the Rev.   , Moderator of Session *ad interim*, to preside on the occasion.

Attested by
, *Session Clerk.*

II.—Annual Meeting of Congregation.

Notice is hereby given that, by appointment of the Session, the Annual Meeting of this Congregation will be held in   on   , the   day of   , at   o'clock, for the purpose of receiving the Annual Report from the Deacons' Court [*or* from the Board of Managers], and of transacting such other business as may be duly brought forward.

Attested by
, *Session Clerk*

III.—Special Meetings of Congregation.

1. Notice is hereby given that, by appointment of the Session, a Meeting of this Congregation will be held in   , on   , the   day of   , at   o'clock, for the purpose of electing new Trustees.

Note.—In this Notice due regard must be had to any provisions on the subject in the Trust or Title-Deeds of the property belonging to, or held on behoof of, the Congregation.

2. Notice is hereby given that, by appointment of the Session, a Meeting of this Congregation will be held in   , on   , the   day of   at   o'clock, for purpose of considering what steps should be taken in obedience to the citation of the Presbytery of   to appear for their interests in connection with a Call which has been addressed to their Minister, the Rev.   , at a Meeting of the aforesaid Presbytery, in   , on   , the   day of   , at   o'clock.

3. Notice is hereby given that, by appointment of the Session, a Meeting of this Congregation will be held in   , on   , the   day of   , at   o'clock, for the purpose of considering the propriety of [*erecting a new church*], and taking such steps as may be deemed expedient or necessary in connection therewith.

IV.—NOTICES FOR THE ELECTION OF ELDERS, OR DEACONS, OR MANAGERS.

1. Notice is hereby given that the Session, having taken into consideration the propriety of adding to the number of Elders [*or* Deacons, *or* Managers] in this Congregation, resolved that it is expedient that at least   additional Elders [*or* Deacons, *or* and   additional Deacons] be appointed, and that the usual steps be taken to procure the nomination and election of such by the Members of the Congregation, on or before the   day of   , 18 .
          Attested by
                              , *Session Clerk*.

Note.—The Minister should here state precisely the mode agreed upon by the Session for ascertaining the choice of the Congregation.

2. Notice is hereby given that the Session of this Congregation appointed *pro tempore* by the Presbytery of   , having considered the propriety of the formation of a permanent Session from the Members of the Congregation, resolved that it is expedient that at least   Elders be apppointed, and that the usual steps be taken for the nomination and election of such by the Members of the Congregation on or before the   day of   , 18 .
          Attested by
                              , *Session Clerk*.

N.—FORMS OF DECLARATIONS.

I.—By the Moderator of Presbytery at the Ordination of a Minister.

In the name and by the authority of this Presbytery, I hereby declare you, Mr. A. B., to be duly ordained to the office of the Ministry of the Gospel, and admitted and inducted into the Pastoral Charge of this Congregation of   , and entitled to all the rights and privileges of that office. In token thereof I give to you the right hand of fellowship in the Lord.

II.—By the Moderator of Presbytery at the Induction of a Minister.

In the name and by the authority of this Presbytery, I hereby declare you, Mr. A. B., to be duly admitted and inducted into the Pastoral Charge of this Congregation of   , and entitled to all the rights and privileges of that office. In token thereof I give to you the right hand of fellowship in the Lord.

III.—By the Moderator of Presbytery at the Admission of a Minister of another Church without a Pastoral Charge.

In the name and by the authority of this Presbytery, I hereby declare you, Mr. A. B., to be admitted as a Minister of the Presbyterian Church of England, without a Pastoral Charge, and entitled to all the rights and privileges of that position, and subject to all the laws of the said Church.

IV.—By the Moderator of Presbytery at the Admission of a Congregation of another Church.

In the name and by the authority of this Presbytery, I hereby declare you, the Members of the Congregation usually assembling in this place, to be received into the Presbyterian Church of England, and entitled to all the rights, and vested with all the privileges, and subject to all the laws of the said Church.

V.—By the Moderator of Presbytery at the Joint-Admission of a Minister and Congregation of another Church.

In the name and by the authority of this Presbytery, I hereby declare you, the Minister and the Members of this Congregation, to be jointly and severally received into the Presbyterian Church of England, and respectively entitled to all the rights, and vested with all the privileges, and subject to all the laws of the said Church.

VI.—By the Moderator of Presbytery at the Licensing of a Preacher.

In the name of the Lord Jesus Christ, the only Head of the Church, and by warrant and appointment of this Presbytery, I do hereby license you to preach the glorious Gospel of the Grace of God, and declare you to be a Probationer for the Ministry of the Presbyterian Church of England. "Give diligence to present thyself approved unto God, a workman that needeth not to be ashamed, handling aright the word of truth." "The Lord bless thee, and keep thee; the Lord make His face to shine upon thee, and be gracious unto thee; the Lord lift up His countenance upon thee, and give thee peace."

VII.—By the Moderator of Session at the Ordination or Induction of Elders or Deacons.

In the name and by the authority of this Session, I hereby declare you, Mr. A. B., duly ordained and admitted [or inducted and admitted] into the office of the Eldership [or Deaconship] in this Congregation, and entitled to all the rights and privileges of that office. In token thereof I give to you the right hand of fellowship in the Lord.

O.—AFFIRMATION BY A WITNESS.

I, A. B., do solemnly declare that I will speak the truth, the whole truth, and nothing but the truth, so far as I shall be asked, and that, in doing so, I am free from malice.

P.—MEMORIAL OR PETITION.

We, the undersigned, residing in the district of   , in the parish of   , which is inadequately supplied with public religious ordinances [or, here state any other fact or facts relating to the Memorial], expressing our appreciation of the principles and services of the Presbyterian Church of England, respectfully request the Presbytery of   , to take our case into their favourable consideration, and to take all needful steps to provide us with supply of public religious ordinances, either by opening a Preaching Station or forming a Congregation in the district in which we reside; and further, in the event of the Presbytery's compliance with our request, we promise our cordial support of the work according to our several ability.

Q.—FORMS OF MINUTES.

A.—OF SESSION.

I.—CONSTITUTION.

At   , the   day of   18 .
The Session met and was constituted.
The Rev.   , Moderator, Messrs.   ,
Elders.
The Minutes of last Meeting were read and confirmed.

II.—BUSINESS.

1.—MODERATOR.

The Session hereby recognises and records the fact that on the   day of   , the Rev.   was ordained by the Presbytery of   to the Office of the Holy Ministry, and admitted as Pastor of this Congregation, and has now for the first time taken his seat as Moderator of Session.

2.—THE LORD'S SUPPER.

a. The Session resolves that the Ordinance of the Lord's Supper shall be observed in this Church on the   day of   , and that public notice thereof be given from the pulpit on the   .

b. The Session resolves that the Ordinance of the Lord's Supper shall be observed in this Church on the [*first*] Lord's Day in [*January, March*, or other month agreed upon], during the currency of the next   months, and that public intimation thereof be duly made to the Congregation.

3. ADMISSION OF COMMUNICANTS.

a. The Moderator reported that the following persons had applied for admission as Communicants for the first time, and that, after examination, he was satisfied as to their Christian knowledge and profession, and recommended that their application be granted, viz.—A. B., etc., etc.

The Session having no ground for questioning the good character of any of these persons, adopts the Moderator's recommendation, hereby admits them to Communion with this Congregation, and places their names on the Communion Roll.

b. Applications for Admission as Communicants on production of Certificates of Church Membership were laid before the Session, viz.—by A. B., from the Church of   ; by C. D., from the Church of   ; etc.

These Certificates having been examined, and found satisfactory, the Session grants the Applications, admits the Members to Communion with this Congregation, and adds their names to the Communion Roll.

4. COMMUNION ROLL.

a. The Session resolves to meet to revise and make up the Communion Roll on   the   day of   , 18   at   o'clock.

b. The Session having revised the Communion Roll *nominatim*, finds as follows, viz.:—That during the past [*six months*, or *year*, as the case may be], [20] names were added by Certificates, and [20] by Examination; that [20] names were removed by Disjunction Certificates, [20] by Death, and [20] by Lapse of Attendance and other causes; and that the Roll now consists of [200] names.

Resolved—That the Roll consisting of the [200] names aforesaid be attested as correct by the Moderator and Clerk, and transmitted to the Presbytery of

c. In view of the Election of a Minister, and of Application for opportunity to give a Call, the Session resolves to meet to revise the Communion Roll up to date, on   , the   day of   , 18   , at   o'clock.

[The Minute of this Meeting may run in such terms as given above: 4 *b*.]

5. REPRESENTATIVE IN PRESBYTERY.

The Session proceeded to elect a Member to represent them in the Presbytery of   , during the next   months.

It was moved, seconded, and agreed to—That A. B., one of their number, be elected for the next   months.

Or, It was moved, seconded, and resolved—That A. B., a Member of the Session of   , be appointed to represent this Session in the Presbytery of during the next   months.

The Clerk was instructed to issue his Commission in common form according to the rules of the Church, and transmit it to the Clerk of Presbytery.

6. REPRESENTATIVE IN SYNOD.

The Session proceeded to elect a Ruling Elder to represent them in the Synod of the Presbyterian Church of England appointed to assemble at   , on the   day of   next.

On the Motion of A. B., seconded by C. D., the Session made choice of E. F., one of their number, to represent them in the Synod aforesaid.

Or, On the Motion of A. B., seconded by C. D., the Session made choice of E. F., a Member of the Session of   to represent this Session in the Synod aforesaid.

The Clerk was instructed to issue his Commission in common form according to the rules of the Church, and transmit it to the Clerk of Synod.

7. Sunday Schools.

a. The Session have made inquiries respecting the district of   , in   ; having ascertained the urgent need of additional provision therein for the religious education of the young; and having found that suitable premises have been secured [or, may be secured] for that purpose in   , unanimously resolved, That a Sunday School be opened in the aforesaid premises, on   , the   day of   , at   o'clock; that A. B. be appointed Superintendent thereof, and C. D., etc., Teachers therein; and that the Members of the Congregation be appealed to for aid in carrying on this work.

b. The Moderator laid on the table and read a letter from Mr. A. B, intimating that in consequence of [*ill health, removal from the district,* or some other cause] he placed his resignation of the Office of Superintendent of the Sunday School [meeting in such a place] in the hands of the Session.

Resolved—That the resignation be accepted [with such expression as the circumstances of the case seem to call for]; *Or*, That the resignation lie on the table, and that Messrs. C. D., E. F., be appointed to confer with Mr. A. B. on the subject, and to report at the next Meeting.

c. The Session appointed Messrs. G. H., I. J., to be visitors of the Sunday School Meeting in [   ], and Messrs. K. L., M. N., to be Visitors of the Sunday School Meeting in [   ] during the next [*six* months], and to report at the Meeting next after the expiration of their appointment.

8. Home Mission Work.

The Session having taken into consideration the religious destitution of the people residing in the district of [   ], and having been assured of the willingness of this Congregation to assist in meeting that destitution, resolved to establish a Mission in said district, and to take such steps as may be necessary for conducting it with efficiency. The Moderator, Messrs. A. B., C. D.

were appointed a Committee to consider and report on the best means of carrying out this resolution.

9. Division of Congregation into Districts.

The Session took into consideration the division of the Congregation into Districts for the Elders, and resolved that it shall, in the meantime, stand as follows:

Districts.		Elders.
No. 1.	[Its name and boundaries.]	Mr. A. B.
No. 2.	[Do. .]	Mr. C. D.
etc.	etc.	etc.

[*In cases where there are Deacons' Courts or Boards of Managers.*]

Further, the Session, in view of the need of a careful superintendence of the Congregation in respect to all its interests, agreed to request a Conference with the Deacons' Court [*or*, Board of Managers], on an early day for the purpose of associating Deacons [*or*, Managers], with the Elders in the oversight of their districts; and they instructed the Clerk to communicate with the Deacons' Court [*or*, Board of Managers] accordingly.

10. Motions.

a. *Notice of Motion.*

Mr. A. B. gave notice of his intention to move at next stated Meeting, in the following terms:—[State the terms of the Motion.]

b. *Motion agreed to.*

Mr. A. submitted the Motion of which he gave Notice at the last Meeting, and moved its adoption, viz. [Give its terms.] The motion was seconded by Mr. C. D., and was unanimously agreed to.

c. *Motion carried on a Division.*

The Session took into consideration the subject of [   ].

It was moved and seconded, That [   ].

It was also moved and seconded, That [   ].

After conversation it was agreed to take the vote. The votes were marked, and it appeared that   members had voted for the first Motion, and   for the second,

so that the   Motion was carried by a majority of
        . Thereupon the Session, in the terms of that Motion, resolve, That [

].

d. *Dissent from a Motion.*

[When one or more Members of Session dissent from a Motion carried, the Minutes of Session may be in such terms as these:—]

From this judgment Mr. A. B. and Mr. C. D. craved leave to enter their Dissent, which was allowed.

[If the Dissent be with Reasons, the Minute may read thus:—]

From this judgment Mr. E. F. and Mr. G. K. dissented for Reasons to be given in due time. [*Or*, for Reasons read and ordered to be kept *in retentis; or*, for the following reasons which were read and allowed to be entered in the Minutes of the Session.]

e. *Dissent and Complaint.**

[If one or more Members dissent and protest for leave to complain to the Presbytery against a Motion which has been carried, the Minute may be in these terms:—]

From this decision, Mr. A. B. and Mr. C. D. dissented, and they protested for leave to complain of it to the Presbytery of   , for the following Reasons, viz.:— [enter the Reasons]. [*Or*, for Reasons to be given to the Clerk in due time.]

The Dissent and Complaint were allowed, and Messrs. E. F., G. K., were appointed to appear before the Presbytery of   , in support of the decision of the Session.

The Clerk was instructed to send Extract Minutes relative to the case to the Presbytery of   .

f. *Appeal.*

The Session took up the case of Mr. A. B., who has been charged with the offence of   . The evidence having been concluded, and Mr. A. B. having been heard in defence, it was moved by Mr. C. D., seconded by Mr. E. F., and agreed to—That the offence charged against Mr. A. B. be found proved. The Moderator having called in Mr. A. B. intimated to him this judgment, against which he protested and appealed to the Presbytery of   .

His appeal was allowed, and extract Minutes were granted to him.

Messrs. C. D., E. F., were appointed to appear before the Presbytery of   , in support of the judgment of the Session.

---

* S e Section IV., page 50.

11. Election and Ordination of Elders.

a. Appointment of Election.

The Session, having taken into consideration the question of adding to the number of Elders, resolved to take steps for that end, and accordingly requested the Moderator to make an intimation next Lord's Day (and, should the Session desire it, on the two successive Lord's Days) to the effect that the election will take place in the following manner, viz. :— [State the mode of election.]

It was agreed that the number to be elected shall be   , and that the Moderator shall intimate the number. It was also agreed that the Moderator should address the people on their duties in this matter, and take occasion to point out the Scriptural qualifications of Elders.

b. Voting at Election.

The Session met for the purpose of carrying out the election of Elders in the manner agreed upon at the meeting on the   day of   .

The Moderator intimated that he had complied with the request of the Session recorded in the Minute now read. [Here let it be stated either that the lists were opened and read and the votes marked, etc., in presence of the Congregation (*or publicly or privately according to resolution*), or that the Session met with the Congregation and proceeded to an election, when motions were made, etc., and the following were elected (*either unanimously or by a majority, as the case may be*), in the following order, the person named first having the greatest number of votes), and so on in the order of votes].

c. Decision of Session on Election.

The Session find that the following persons have been elected by the Congregation to the Eldership, viz. :— Messrs. A. B., C. D., E. F., etc.

It was agreed that the election of the aforesaid Messrs.   , be sustained.

It was agreed that the Moderator should ascertain the willingness of the aforesaid Messrs.   to accept office.

d. Report of Moderator on Elders-Elect.

The Moderator reported that he had communicated with the persons whose election to the Eldership in this Congregation had been sustained as to their acceptance of the office, and that the following had agreed to accept, viz. :—Messrs A. B., C. D., E. F., etc.

e. Appointment of Ordination [and Admission] of Elders.

The Session appoint the ordination of Messrs. A. B., C. D., etc. [and the admission of Mr. R. S., already ordained to the Eldership in another Congregation], to take place in the presence of the Congregation on the   , after public worship in the   , and they direct an edict to this effect to be served in common form on the   day of   , giving notice to the people that if any of them have any objections to state to the character or doctrinal opinions of any of the aforesaid persons, they are required to state the same at a meeting of Session to be held in   , on   , the   day of   , at   o'clock, with declaration that unless such objections be substantiated at said meeting, the ordination [and admission] will be carried out.

f. Ordination [and Admission] of Elders.

The Moderator reported that the Edict of the Ordination of Messrs. A. B., C. D., E. F., etc. [and of the Admission of Messrs. G. H., I. J., etc.] to the Eldership in this Congregation has been duly served. No objections having been offered to the character and conduct of the aforesaid Messrs.   , the Session resolved to proceed to their Ordination [and Admission]. The Moderator put to Messrs. A. B., C. D., etc., the questions appointed to be put to Elders before their admission to office, to which they all gave satisfactory answers.

Whereupon, after prayer, the Moderator, in name of the Session, did declare Messrs.   , to be duly ordained to the Office of Eldership, and admitted to the exercise of the same in this Congregation, and to all the rights and privileges belonging thereto. In token thereof he gave to them the right hand of fellowship in the Lord, as did also the other members of the Session. The Moderator addressed the newly-admitted Elders and the Congregation on their respective duties.

Public worship having been concluded, and the Session continuing their meeting, the names of the newly admitted Elders were added to the roll of the Session, and the Session Clerk was instructed to intimate the same to the Clerk of the Deacons' Court for communication.

12.—ELECTION AND ORDINATION OF DEACONS.

As the course followed in the Election and Ordination of Deacons is in principle the same as in the case of Elders, the Minutes of Session relative thereto may be in corresponding terms.

13.—Election of a Minister.

The Session having taken into consideration the desirableness of ascertaining whether the Congregation are yet prepared to proceed to the choice of a Minister to fill up the vacancy in the pastorate, it was moved, seconded and agreed to—That a meeting of the Congregation for the above purpose be held in the Church, on   , the   day of   , at   o'clock; the Rev. A. B., Moderator *pro tem.*, to preside on the occasion. Further, the Session direct that notice of this Meeting be publicly given to the Congregation on the   day of   .

14.—Application for the giving of a Call to a Minister.

The Moderator reported that the Meeting of the Congregation appointed to be held on the   , relative to the election of a Minister, had taken place, and that it appeared that the Congregation were unanimously [*or*, by a considerable majority] in favour of giving a Call to a Minister.

The Session having considered the Report, it was moved, seconded, and agreed to—That they authorise the Moderator, in their name, to inform the Presbytery of   , at its next Meeting, that this Congregation is ripe for the election of a Minister, and to request that Reverend Court to grant an opportunity for the giving of a Call on an early day.

B.—OF DEACONS' COURT OR BOARD OF MANAGERS.

1.—Constitution.

At   , the   day of   18   :
The Deacons' Court (*or Board of Managers*) met: *Sederunt*; The Rev.   ;
Messrs. A. B., C. D., etc., *Elders*; Messrs. I. M., N. O., etc., *Deacons (Managers)*.

[In the absence of the Minister, Mr.   was called to the chair.] The meeting was constituted with prayer.

2.—Business.

1. *Additional Elders and Deacons (or Managers).*

The Minutes of the last meeting were read and confirmed.

An Extract Minute of   Session was laid on the table, from which it appeared that Mr.

and Mr.   , etc., had been admitted as Elders of this Congregation on the   day of   .

Another Extract Minute was read, by which it appeared that Mr.   and Mr.   , etc., etc., had been admitted as Deacons of this Congregation on the   day of   .

The Deacons' Court (*or Board of Managers*) instruct the Clerk to add the names of these persons to the Roll as Members.

Another Extract Minute was read, showing that Mr.   had ceased to be an Elder, and Mr.   to be a Deacon (*or Manager*) of this Congregation.

The Court (*or Board*) instruct the Clerk to remove the names of these persons from the Roll.

2. *Church Officer.*

The Deacons' Court (*or Board of Managers*) taking into consideration the vacancy in the office of Church Officer of this Congregation, and the following applications for the office, resolve to appoint, and hereby do appoint, Mr.   to be the Church Officer. They resolve that his salary shall be   , and appoint the Clerk and Mr.   to confer with him as to his duties, and to report.

3. *Districts.*

The Court (*or Board*) resolve to divide the Congregation anew into districts, to be severally assigned to the Deacons, as follows:—District 1, Mr.   , etc.

4. *Sustentation Fund.*

The Court (*or Board*) instruct each of the Deacons (*or Managers*) to take charge of and hold himself responsible for arrangements for the ingathering of the Sustentation Fund in his district, and they appoint Mr.   to be Treasurer for that Fund, Mr.   remaining Treasurer for the Local Funds, and Mr.   for the Foreign Missions Fund.

5. *Supplement to Stipend.*

The Deacons' Court (*or Board of Managers*), finding that, after deduction of sums requisite for the claims recognised as primary by the Act of Synod, there remains a surplus in the Local fund of £   s.   d., took into consideration the question how far it was reasonable to supplement (or add to the supplement to) the Minister's stipend, and resolved to grant him the sum of £   s.   d. out of the surplus.

6. *Special Collection.*

The Deacons' Court (*or Board of Managers*) resolved that a special collection be made on the   day of   , for the relief of poor members of the Congregation at this season.

7. *Motions.*

It was moved and seconded, That

It was also moved and seconded, That

8. *Dissent.*

The votes having been taken, the [1st] Motion was carried by a majority of   to   . From this judgment Mr.   dissented for the following reasons, viz.,—1, etc. 2, etc. 3, etc. Mr.   adhered to the Dissent.

(N.B.—*When reasons are produced immediately along with the Dissent in any Church Court, they are made part of the Minute.*)

9. *Seat Letting.*

The Court (*or Board*) directed intimation to be made next Lord's Day of the seat-letting for the ensuing half-year; and they appointed the following Committee to collect the seat-rents, to let vacant sittings, and to allocate sittings to the poor who are unable to pay for the same—viz., Messrs.   and   , with the Clerk and Congregational Treasurer—Mr.   , Convener.

10. *Audit of Accounts.*

The auditors appointed at last Meeting reported that they had examined the Treasurer's accounts, had compared the same with the vouchers, and had found them correct. Of these accounts, the following is an abstract:—(*Here take it in.*) The Court (*or Board*) sustained the report, and resolved that these Accounts, with the abstract thereof, be laid before the Congregation by the Treasurer, with such explanations as he may deem necessary at the Annual Meeting to be held on the   day of   .

11. *Cleaning and Repairs of Church.*

The attention of the Court (*or Board*) having been called to the necessity of cleaning the church, and making sundry repairs thereof, appointed Messrs. A B., C. D., etc., a Committee with full powers to obtain estimates of the cost of such cleaning and repairs as they may determine upon, to accept the estimate which they deem most favourable, and to take care that the work be carried out accordingly.

12. *Addition to Stipend.*

Pursuant to notice given at last stated Meeting, Mr. A. B. moved—That, subject to the approval of the Congregation, the Stipend of the Minister be increased by [£100] *per annum.*

The motion was seconded by Mr. C. D., and agreed to.

C.—OF CONGREGATIONAL MEETINGS.

1.—Of Meeting relative to a New Church.

At   , the   day of   18 , the Congregation of   Church met by appointment of the Session for the purpose of considering whether steps should be taken for the erection of a new Church.

The Rev. A. B. having taken the Chair, the Meeting was opened with prayer.

The circumstances and requirements of the case having been spoken to by several Members, it was moved by Mr. A. B., seconded by Mr. C. D., and agreed to—That this Congregation deem it necessary to proceed to the erection of a new Church, and for this purpose appoint the following Committee, viz.: Messrs. E. F., G. H., etc., with full powers to select a suitable Site, to determine on Plans and Estimates, the latter not to exceed [£2000], to obtain Subscriptions, to take all steps requisite for carrying out the work to completion, and to report thereon from time to time as they shall see cause.

2.—Of Meeting relative to the Election of a Minister.

At   , the   day of   , 18 , the Congregation of   Church met by appointment of the Session to ascertain whether they should proceed to the Election of a Minister.

The Rev. A. B., Moderator of Session *pro tem.*, took the Chair, and the Meeting was opened with devotional exercises.

It was moved by Mr. C. D., and seconded by Mr. E. F.—That a Call be addressed to the Rev. G. H., Minister of the Gospel.

It was moved by Mr. I. J., and seconded by Mr. K. L—That a Call be addressed to Mr. M. N., Preacher of the Gospel.

It was moved by Mr. O. P., and seconded by Mr. Q. R.—That procedure in a Call be delayed, and that Messrs.

be invited to preach in this Church, on the   , and on the   , respectively.

After deliberation the Votes of the Members were duly taken on the aforesaid Motions, when the [*first*] Motion was carried by a majority of [50] votes, and the Congregation resolved accordingly, and agreed to request the Session to apply to the Presbytery of   , for an opportunity to give a Call to a Minister on an early day.

D.—OF PRESBYTERY.

Ordinary Meeting.

I. CONSTITUTION.

At   the   day   of   18
At which time and place the Presbytery of
    met, and was constituted with prayer.
Sederunt—The Rev.   , *Moderator.*
Messrs. A. B., C. D., etc., *Ministers.*
Messrs. L. M., N. O., etc., *Elders.*
The Minutes of the last ordinary meeting were read and sustained.

II. BUSINESS.

1.—Elders' Commissions.

Elders' commissions were received from the Sessions of   , etc., in favour respectively of Mr.   , Mr.   , etc. Said commissions, being in due form, were sustained, and the names were added to the roll; and Messrs.   being present, took their seats accordingly.

2.—Election of Moderator.

The Moderator's term of office having expired, the Presbytery proceeded to the election of a Moderator for the next [*six*] months.

Whereupon, it was moved by Mr. A. B., seconded by Mr. C. D., and agreed to—That Mr. E. F., Minister at   , be appointed Moderator for the next [*six*] months.

Mr. E. F., being present, Mr. G. H., the retiring Moderator, left the chair, which was taken accordingly by Mr. E. F.

3.—Appointment of Committees.

a. On Sustentation Fund.

It was moved, seconded, and agreed to:—That the following be a committee to watch over the interests of the Sustentation Fund within the bounds, and to report thereon to the Presbytery at each ordinary meeting, viz., Messrs.   , *Ministers* ; Messrs.   *Elders* ; Mr.   , *Convener*.

b. On Sunday Schools.

On the Motion of Mr. A. B., seconded by Mr. C. D., the following were appointed a Committee to visit and report on the Sunday Schools within the bounds, to make such arrangements as they may deem necessary for the delivery of a course of Lectures to Sunday School Teachers, and to inquire if any, and, if so, what additional steps should be taken to promote the religious instruction of the young leaving Sabbath Schools.

c. On Church Extension.

(1.) Mr. A. B., having brought before the Presbytery the large increase in the population in the town [*or* towns, or district of   ] within the bounds, and to the great need of better provision for the supply of Gospel Ordinances therein, it was resolved that the following be appointed a Committee for the purpose of promoting Church Extension within the aforesaid towns [*or* towns, or district of   ] by such means as may seem to them most expedient, and reporting thereon from time to time, viz.:—Messrs. A. B., C. D., etc., *Ministers* ; Messrs. E. F., G. H., etc., *Elders* ; Mr. K. L., *Convener*.

(2.) Mr.   , on behalf of the Church Extension Committee, reported that they had made inquiries respecting the population and the religious necessities of the [*town, district, parish*, or *village*, or otherwise], and requested power to open a preaching station there on an early day.

Resolved—That the request be granted, that   be recognised as a preaching station within the bounds, and that, in the meantime, the Church Extension Committee   be authorised to provide for it a supply of preaching, and to report.

4.—Call to a Minister.

a. Call to be given.

Mr. A. B., Moderator *ad interim* of the Session of   Church, reported that the Congregation were ripe for the election of a Minister, and on behalf of the Session and Congregation he requested the Presbytery to grant opportunity for giving a Call to a Minister on an early day.

(1.) It was moved, seconded, and agreed to:—That the request be complied with, and that the Rev.   be appointed to preach and preside at the giving of a Call to a Minister in   Church, on   the   day of   , at   o'clock, and that intimation thereof be made to the Congregation by the officiating Minister on the   day of   .

(2.) It was moved, seconded, and agreed to—That the request be granted, and that the Presbytery do meet in   Church on   , the   day of   , at   o'clock, at the giving of a Call to a Minister, and to take such steps in connection therewith as may be deemed expedient. Notice of said Meeting to be duly given to the Congregation on the   .

b. Call sustained.

(1.) The Rev.   reported that he had fulfilled the appointment of the Presbytery to preach and preside at the giving of a Call to a Minister in   Church [London], on the   day of   , and he laid on the table a Call which had been duly addressed by the Congregation there to Mr. A. B., Preacher of the Gospel, signed by [100] Members and a Form of Concurrence therewith, signed by [50] Adherents.

Resolved—That the Call be sustained, and that the Clerk be instructed to give intimation thereof to Mr. A. B., and to request his answer to the Call in time to be laid before the Presbytery at its Meeting on the   day of   .

(2.) The Rev.   reported that he had fulfilled the appointment of the Presbytery to preach and preside at the giving of a Call to a Minister at   , on the   day of   ; and he laid on the table a Call which had been duly addressed by the Congregation there to the Rev.   Minister of   Church, in   , signed by [100] Members, and a Form of Concurrence therewith signed by [50] Adherents.

Resolved—That the Call be sustained, and that the usual steps be taken for prosecuting the translation of the Rev.   from   to   . Mr. A. B. and Mr. C. D. were appointed Commissioners to the Presbytery of   to prosecute the Call to its issue.

(3.) At the close of public worship the Moderator stated to the Congregation the special object of the Meeting and the Order of Procedure.

The Form of a Call to a Minister was read by the Clerk.

It was moved by Mr. A. B., seconded by Mr. C. D., and unanimously agreed to—That the name of Mr. E. F., Minister at   , be inserted in the Call now read.

The name of Mr. E. F. was accordingly inserted in the Call, which was signed in the presence of the Presbytery by [200] Members, and a Form of Concurrence therewith by [60] Adherents.

It was moved, seconded, and resolved—That the Call now on the table be sustained, and that the usual steps be taken for prosecuting the transference of Mr. E. F. from   to   , and Messrs. G. H. and I. J. were appointed Commissioners for that purpose to the Presbytery of   .

[In the case of the Call being to a Probationer, the Minute may be in such terms as above (1).]

c. Call accepted.

(1.) The Clerk laid on the table and read a letter from Mr. A. B., Preacher of the Gospel, intimating his willingness to accept the Call which has been given to him by the Congregation of   , to become their Pastor.

Resolved—That the Moderator be authorised to prescribe to Mr. A. B., the requisite subjects of trials with a view to his Ordination to the Office of the Ministry, and to his Admission to the pastoral charge of the Congregation of   , and that said trials be taken at a Meeting of the Presbytery on the   day of   , at   o'clock.

(2.) The Clerk laid on the table and read a letter from the Rev. A. B., intimating that, having resigned his charge at   , and having been duly loosed therefrom by the Presbytery of   , he accepted the Call which had been addressed to him by the Congregation at   to become their Pastor.

Extract Minutes of the proceedings of said Presbytery relative to Mr. A. B.'s resignation were laid on the table and read.

d. Call declined.

The Clerk laid on the table and read a letter from Mr. A. B., Probationer, intimating that, after careful consideration, he considered it to be his duty to decline the Call which had been given to him to the pastoral charge of the Congregation at   . The aforesaid Call was set aside.

5. Transference of a Minister.

a. Mr. A. B., as Commissioner of the Presbytery, to prosecute the Call from the Congregation at   , to the Rev.   Minister at   , reported that the Presbytery of   , at their meeting on the   day of   , had agreed to the transference of the Rev.   from   to   . He laid on the table Extract Minutes of the proceedings of the Presbytery of   in the case, which were read.

b. The Presbytery proceeded to consider the Call which had been received from the Congregation at   to the Rev. A. B. to become their Pastor.

The following Papers relative to the case were read, viz.:—(1.) Extract Minutes of the Presbytery of   . (2.) Reasons for the Transference of the Rev. A. B from   to   . (3.) Answers to the aforesaid Reasons. [If there be other Papers they should be noted.]

The Parties were called, and the following appeared, viz.:—Mr. A. D., for the Presbytery   ; Mr. E. F., for the Session of   ; Mr. G. H., for the Congregation; on the other side, Mr. I. J., for the Session of   ; Mr. K. L., for the Congregation of   . The Rev. A. B. appeared for himself.

Parties having been heard, were removed from the bar.

The Presbytery united in prayer.

It was moved, seconded, and agreed to:—That the transference craved is expedient, and that the Call now on the table be put into the hands of the Rev. A. B.

The Moderator accordingly placed the Call in the hands of Mr.   , who intimated his acceptance thereof.

Wherefore, the Presbytery did, and hereby do, resolve that the Rev. A. B. be transferred from the pastoral charge of the Congregation of   , to that of the Congregation of   , in the Presbytery of   , and that he be instructed to await the orders of said Presbytery of   for his Induction into the pastorate of said Congregation of

6.—ORDINATION OF A MINISTER.

a. Appointment of Ordination.

Mr. A. B., Probationer, under Call to the pastorate of the Congregation of   , having passed the prescribed trials for Ordination with approval, the Presbytery resolved to meet for his Ordination to the Office of the Holy Ministry of the Gospel, and to his admission into the pastorate of the aforesaid Congregation, in the Church of   , on the   day   , at   o'clock. Further, the Presbytery appoint the

Rev. C. D. to preach on the occasion, and the Rev. E. F. to preside at the Ordination, and to address the Minister and the Congregation; and they direct the Edict of Ordination to be served in common form according to the rules of the Church, on the   day of   .

b. *Act of Ordination.*

[When the Ordination takes place at a Meeting *in hunc effectum*, the Minute recording the Constitution of the Presbytery should state that it was such a Meeting.]

The Edict of Ordination was returned certified as having been duly served.

The hour for public worship having come, objections to the character or the teaching of Mr. A. B. were called for, and none were offered.

Whereupon, the Presbytery entered the Church, where public worship was conducted by the Rev. C. D., and a sermon preached on   .

The Moderator put to Mr. A. B. the questions appointed to be put before Ordination, and received satisfactory answers thereto. Wherefore, the Presbytery, by solemn prayer to God, and by the laying on of hands, ordained Mr. A. B. to the Office of the Holy Ministry of the Gospel; and thereafter, the Moderator, in the name and by the authority of the Presbytery, declared Mr. A. B. duly admitted and inducted into the pastoral charge of this Church and Congregation; and, along with the Brethren, gave him the right hand of fellowship.

The Moderator addressed Mr. A. B. and the Congregation on their respective duties.

At the close of the service Mr. A. B. received a cordial welcome from the people of his Charge, and his name was added to the Roll of the Presbytery.

7.—INDUCTION OF A MINISTER.

a. *Appointment of Induction.*

Resolved—That the Presbytery do meet at   , on the   day of   , at   o'clock, for the Induction of the Rev.   into the pastoral charge of the Church and Congregation of   .

The Presbytery appoint the Rev.   to preach on the occasion, and the Rev.   to preside at the Induction, and to address the Minister and the Congregation; and they direct the Edict of Induction to be served in common form, according to the rules of the Church, on the   day of   .

b. *Act of Induction.*

The edict of the Induction of the Rev.   was returned certified as having been duly served.

Objections to the character or the teaching of the Rev.   , were called for, and none offered. Whereupon, the Presbytery entered the Church, where public worship was conducted by the Rev.   , and a sermon preached on   .

The Moderator put to the Rev.   the Questions appointed to be put to Ministers before Induction, and received satisfactory answers.

Whereupon, after solemn prayer to God, he did, in the name and by the authority of the Presbytery, declare Mr.   to be admitted and inducted into the Pastoral Charge of this Church and Congregation, and entitled to all the rights and privileges belonging to that office; and, along with the members of the Presbytery, gave him the right hand of fellowship. The Moderator addressed the newly-inducted Minister and the Congregation on their respective duties.

At the close of the service, Mr.   's name was added to the Roll of the Presbytery.

8.—Overture to Synod.

a. *Notice of Overture.*

Mr. A. B. gave notice of his intention to propose, at next Ordinary Meeting, that the following Overture be transmitted to the Synod, viz.: [*Here give the terms of the Overture*].

b. *Consideration of Overture.*

(1) According to notice given, Mr.   moved that the following Overture be transmitted to the Synod, viz.: [*Here insert the Overture*].

This Motion was seconded by Mr.   .

It was moved as an Amendment by Mr.   ,—That the Overture now on the table be not transmitted.

This Motion was seconded by Mr.   .

After reasoning, the Presbytery resolved to go to the Vote—the Question being, *Transmit,* or *Not transmit;* when there voted, *Transmit,* 25; *Not transmit,* 12; wherefore the Presbytery resolved that the Overture be transmitted, and it was transmitted accordingly; and Mr.   and Mr.   were appointed to appear in support of it before the Synod.

(2) Pursuant to resolution adopted at last Ordinary Meeting, the Presbytery took up the Overture on [*Presby-*

terian Union] transmitted by the Synod, viz.: [*Here insert the Overture*].

It was moved, seconded, and agreed to—That the Overture be approved.

The Clerk was accordingly instructed to give an Extract Minute of this decision as the Return of this Presbytery to the Synod on the Overture aforesaid.

9.—REFERENCE.

a. *Reference from Session.*

(1) There was laid on the table a Reference from the Session of   , for advice on the following point or points [*These should be here distinctly stated*], in the case of [*The case should be distinctly stated*].

Extract relative Minutes of said Session were read, and Mr. A. B., who had been duly appointed to state the Reference, was heard.

Resolved—That the Reference be sustained, that the Session of   be advised in the following terms, viz.: [*Here give the terms of advice*], and be instructed to proceed in the whole case according to the Rules of the Church.

(2) There was laid on the table a Reference from the Session of   , for judgment in the case of Mr. A. B. charged with the offence of [*State the offence*], and in regard to which they had in an orderly manner completed the proof.

Extract Minutes of the Session relative to the case were read; the Evidence taken by the Session was laid on the table; and Mr. C. D., who had been appointed to state the Reference and give necessary explanations, was heard.

Resolved—That the Presbytery sustain the Reference, adjourn the further consideration of the case to a Special Meeting to be held on the   day of   , at   o'clock, and summon Mr. A. B. to appear for his interests on that day.

b. *Reference from Presbytery.*

The Presbytery resumed consideration of the case of [*Here state the case*], and further heard parties concerned in it.

It was moved, seconded, and agreed to—That, in view of the special difficulties with which the case is surrounded and the important interests involved in it, the Presbytery resolve to refer it *simpliciter* to the Synod. Further—That an Extract Minute of this Reference, and all the Papers connected with the case, be transmitted to the Synod. Further—That all the parties in the case be duly warned to appear before that Court for their interests, and that Messrs. A. B., C. D., be appointed Commissioners to explain to the Synod the matter referred, and the reasons for the Reference.

10.—APPEAL.

a. *Appeal from Session.*

The Presbytery took an Appeal by Mr. A. B. against a judgment of the Session of   .

Minutes of said Session and Papers relative to the case were laid on the table and read.

The parties having been called, Messrs. C. D., E. F., appeared for the Session, and Mr. A. B. appeared for himself.

The parties having been heard, were removed from the bar.

Whereupon, it was moved by Mr. G. H., and seconded by Mr. L. M.—That the Appeal be sustained, and the judgment of the Session of   be reversed.

It was moved as an amendment by Mr. N. O., and seconded by P. Q.—That the Appeal be dismissed, and the judgment of the Session of   be confirmed.

After reasoning, the Presbytery went to the vote, and there voted for the Motion [15], and for the Amendment [12].

Wherefore the Presbytery resolved in terms of the Motion.

b. *Appeal from Presbytery.*

There was laid before the Presbytery a Petition from the Session of   Church,   , craving the sanction of the Presbytery to the erection of a new Church for their Congregation on a site at [*Describe the locality of the site*]. Mr. A. B. and Mr. C. D., Commissioners from the Session, were heard in support of the prayer of the Petition, and explained the reasons which led to the selection of the site.

It was moved, and seconded—That the prayer of the Petition be granted.

It was moved as an Amendment, and seconded—That the prayer of the Petition be not granted.

After reasoning, the Presbytery proceeded to the vote, when [10] voted for the Amendment and [5] for the Motion.

This judgment having been intimated by the Moderator, Mr. A. B. and Mr. C. D., Commissioners from the Session aforesaid, protested and appealed against it to the Synod, for reasons to be given in due time.

The Appeal was allowed, and Messrs. E. F., etc., were appointed to appear before the Synod in support of the judgment of the Presbytery.

11.—Dissent and Complaint.*

a. *From Session.*

The Presbytery took up a Dissent and Complaint of Mr. A. B. and Mr. C. D., Members of the Session of   Church, against the proceedings of said Session in the case of [*Here state the case exactly*].

Extract Minutes of Session relative to the case were read, as were also Minutes of Session appointing Mr. E. F. and Mr. G. H., to appear in support of the judgment of the Session.

The Complainers and the Commissioners were heard.

It was moved and seconded—That the Dissent and Complaint be sustained, and the judgment of the Session be reversed.

It was moved as an Amendment, and seconded—That the Dissent and Complaint be dismissed, and the judgment of the Session be confirmed.

The Presbytery, after reasoning, went to the vote, when [6] voted for Amendment, and [12] for the Motion, and the Presbytery resolved accordingly in the terms of the Motion.

b. *From Presbytery.*

[In such a case as that given in *a*, a Member of the Court may dissent and complain against the judgment given. So also in regard to any decision arrived at. In these cases, after the record of the process which led up to judgment, the Minute may be in the following form:—]

From which judgment Mr. K. L. dissented and protested for leave to complain to the Synod, and promised to give in reasons in due time.

The Dissent and Complaint were allowed, and Messrs. M. N. and O. P. were appointed to appear before the Synod in defence of the judgment of the Presbytery.

12.—Visitation of Congregations.

The Presbytery having taken into consideration the state of religion within the bounds, the desirableness of becoming more fully acquainted with the spiritual life and work of the Congregations under its care, and the need of strengthening the hands of the Ministers and other Office-Bearers for the performance of their sacred duties, resolve that Presbyterial Visitation of the Congregations be entered upon; and, for this purpose, appoint a committee to consider and report to next Ordinary Meeting on the following points, viz: (1) The order of rotation in which the Congregations should be visited. (2) The specific subjects of inquiry and attention to be brought before the Congregations. (3) The special religious ser-

---

* See Section IV., page 50.

vices to be held at the Visitations. And (4), Generally, such other matters as they may deem expedient to bring before the Presbytery with a view to the most efficient conduct of the Visitation.

The Committee to consist of Messrs.   , *Ministers ;* Messrs.   , *Elders ;* Mr.   *Convener.*

13.—PREACHING STATIONS.

(1.) Mr. A. B., *Convener*, reported from the Committee appointed at last Meeting to consider the Memorial signed by [100] persons resident at   , for the opening of a Preaching Station. The report was to the effect that the Committee had met with the Memorialists, had visited the locality named in the Memorial, had inquired as to the population of the district and the provision in it for Public Worship and the Preaching of the Gospel, and had agreed cordially to recommend that the prayer of Memorialists be granted.

Resolved—That the Report of the Committee be adopted, that a Preaching Station be opened at   on the   day of   , and that, in the meantime, it be placed under the Sessional Charge of the neighbouring Session of   .

(2.) Pursuant to Notice given at last Ordinary Meeting, Mr. A. B. moved—That application be made to the Synod at its Meeting to be held in   , in   next, to grant power to this Presbytery, when it shall see cause so to do, to raise the Preaching Station at   , to the status of a regularly sanctioned Congregation.

The Motion was seconded by Mr. C. D., and agreed to; and Mr. A. B. was appointed to appear before the Synod in support of the application.

Meeting pro re natâ.

1.—CONSTITUTION.

At,   , the   day of   , 18   .

At which time and place the Presbytery of   met *pro re natâ.*

Sederunt ; The Rev.   , *Moderator ;* Messrs.   , *Ministers ;* Messrs.   , *Elders.*

2.—BUSINESS.

The circular convening the meeting was read.

The Moderator stated the circumstances which had led him to call the meeting.

It was moved, seconded, and agreed to—That the conduct of the Moderator in calling the meeting be approved.

There were laid on the table and read Extract Minutes of the proceedings of the Presbytery of   relative to a Call from the Congregation at   to the Rev.   , Minister of   . The Call, signed by   members and   adherents, was also laid on the table.

Resolved—That the Call, with relative papers, do lie on the table, and that the Session and Congregation of   be cited to appear for their interests in connection with it at the next ordinary meeting, on the   day of   , at   o'clock; with certification that if they do not appear they shall be held as consenting to the transference of the Rev.   , from   to   .

The Sederunt was closed with prayer.

Meetings in Cases of Discipline.

1.—APPOINTMENT OF COMMITTEE OF INQUIRY IN A CASE OF FAMA AGAINST A MINISTER OR PROBATIONER.

At   , the   day of   , 18 , which day the Presbytery of   met, and was constituted. The Presbytery being alone, it was stated by a Member of Court that certain very unpleasant reports were prevailing in regard to the character of Mr.   , Preacher of the Gospel within their bounds (or their brother, Mr.   , Minister of the Congregation at   ). Whereupon the Presbytery, after due consideration of the same, appointed the following Members, viz.:—Messrs. A. B., C. D., etc., a Committee to make further inquiry into the nature of the *fama* now prevailing against the said   , and to report to the Presbytery at their next Meeting as to the procedure which it may be proper to adopt in this matter.

2.—APPOINTMENT OF PRESBYTERIAL VISITATION.

The Presbytery having taken into their serious consideration the matter brought before them by Mr. A. B., respecting their brother, the Rev. C. D., Minister at   , did, and hereby do, appoint a visitation of the Congregation of   , to take place on   day of   next, that the Elders and Communicants of said Congregation may be examined respecting the rumours now prevailing in regard to their Minister. The Presbytery instruct Mr.   to preach on that occasion, and they further appoint Mr.   to preach in the Church of   , the   day of   , and to give due intimation of said Meeting of Presbytery to all concerned.*

---

* A reasonable time must elapse between the Intimation and the Meeting of the Presbytery.

3.—Petition for Inquiry.

The Presbytery being met, etc. Appeared Mr.   , and presented a Petition, signed by certain persons, signing themselves heads of families in the Congregation of   , and Members of the   Church there, praying the Presbytery to inquire into certain reports now prevalent in regard to Mr.   , Minister of said Congregation (the particular charge alleged must be stated). The Presbytery being alone, resolved, after due deliberation, that the Petition should lie on the table till their next ordinary Meeting, then to be taken into consideration, and (should the person accused be absent) they appointed their Clerk to give intimation thereof to the said Mr.

INDICTMENT.

1.—Indictment given in by Members of a Congregation.

Appeared Mr. A. B., Mr. C. D., etc., who gave in an Indictment against Mr. R. S., Minister of   , which was authenticated by the signatures of the Moderator and Clerk, the tenor whereof follows (*here take it in*). The Presbytery, having considered said Indictment, order a copy thereof, and of the list of witnesses annexed thereto, to be served on the said Mr.   , and direct their officer to cite him to compear before the Presbytery to answer the same at their next ordinary meeting, to be held on   day of   next, at   o'clock; said citation to be made ten free days at least before said Meeting.

a. *Relevancy of Indictment.*

The Presbytery proceeded to the Indictment laid on the table at the Meeting held on the   day of   , against the Rev. R. S., Minister of   .

The Presbytery officer returned execution of citation against the said Mr. R. S., properly attested, bearing that he had, on the   day of   last, regularly served the said Mr. R. S. with a copy of the Indictment and list of witnesses, and duly summoned him to appear before the Presbytery this day, to answer the same.

Mr.   being called appeared. Mr.   attended on behalf of Messrs.   , by whom the Indictment was given in.

The Indictment having been read over, the following defences were given in on the part of Mr.   (*here take them in*).

Parties were then heard on the relevancy of the Indictment; and on being removed, the Presbytery did, and hereby do, find the major proposition of the Indictment relevant; they also find the articles of the minor proposition relevant.

Parties being called in, this decision was intimated to them.

b. *Probation of Indictment resolved upon.*

The Presbytery having resolved to proceed to a proof of the charges in the Indictment, appointed their next Meeting to be held at   , on the   day of   for this purpose; and they authorised and empowered their officer to summon such witnesses in the list appended to said Indictment, as to the libellers may seem meet, to appear in said place, on that day, to give evidence in the cause, and they appointed their Clerk to issue their edict for that purpose. Parties were summoned *apud acta* to attend said meeting.

c. *Probation of Indictment gone into.*

Pursuant to resolution adopted at Meeting held on the   day of   , the Presbytery entered on probation of the Indictment against the Rev. R. S.

The following witnesses on the part of the prosecution were examined, viz:—Messrs. A. B., C. D., etc.

[Their evidence should be recorded.]

The defender offered an exculpatory proof, which was allowed. He also tendered a list of witnesses for examination, and warrant for their due citation was granted.

Resolved—That the Presbytery meet to proceed further in the case on the   day of   , at   o'clock.

In furtherance of resolution come to at the Meeting on the   day of   , the Presbytery proceeded to receive exculpatory proof in the case of the Indictment against the Rev. R. S.

The following witnesses were examined, viz.:—Messrs. A. B., C. D., etc.

[Their evidence should be recorded.]

The exculpatory proof being finished, parties were heard on the evidence, viz.:—Mr. A. B. on the part of those by whom the Indictment was given in, and the Rev. R. S. on his own part.

d. *Judgment upon the Indictment.*

Probation in the case being concluded, the Presbytery, after solemn prayer to God, proceeded to give judgment.

It was moved by Mr. A. B., seconded by Mr. C. D., and agreed to—That all the Counts in the Indictment now on the table against the Rev. R. S. be found proven. [*Or*, that Counts I. and IV. be found *proven*, and Counts II. and III. be found *not proven*.]

[The Presbytery then proceeds to decide the censure required in the case, and the censure is pronounced and carried into effect according to the rules of the Church, provided no Appeal be taken to the Synod.]

The Presbytery having had under their consideration the Indictment, at the instance of   against Mr.   , Minister of the Congregation at   , which set forth, etc., and the citation of the said   —his compearance, his answers to the said Indictment against him—the proof adduced—and having found the same relevant by the acts and practices of this Church, to infer deposition, as also the articles of the said complaint, sufficiently proved by the depositions of the witnesses and other proof adduced, viz., that (*here narrate the charges found proven*) as the proof adduced bears. Therefore the Presbytery did, by their vote, depose the said   , like as they hereby do, in the name of the Lord Jesus Christ, the alone King and Head of His Church, and by virtue of the power and authority committed by Him to them, depose the said   from the office of the Holy Ministry; prohibiting and discharging him to exercise the same, or any part thereof, in all time coming, under the pain of the gravest censures of the Church.

Previously to the Moderator pronouncing the solemn sentence of deposition, prayer is offered by one of the brethren.*

2. INDICTMENT BY PRESBYTERY.

Resolved on.

The Presbytery having received the Report of the Committee appointed to inquire into the *fama* prevalent against the Rev. A. B., and their recommendation to proceed in the case by way of Indictment, resolved as follows, viz.:—That the Report of the Committee be received, and their recommendation adopted, and that the following be appointed a Committee to draw up form of said Indictment, and to lay the same before the Presbytery at a Meeting to be held on the   day of   .

b. Adopted.

The Rev. C. D., Convener of the Committee appointed to prepare a form of Indictment against the Rev. A. B., laid on the table the form of Indictment prepared.

The said form having been read and considered, the Presbytery decided as follows, viz.:—

---

* Sentence of deposition must in all cases be reported to the Synod; and the Synod alone can pronounce sentence of deposition on a Minister in his absence.

The Presbytery hereby approve generally of the form of Indictment prepared by their Committee against Mr.   , Minister at   . They resolve to consider its relevancy, and the propriety of serving it, at a Meeting of Presbytery to be held at   on the   day of   , at   o'clock. They hereby instruct their officer to summon Mr.   in regular form to attend said Meeting, and instruct their Clerk to transmit to him a copy of the proposed Indictment, and of the Minute now agreed to regarding it, in such time as to give him full ten days' notice.

c. *Relevancy of Indictment.*

The Presbytery took up the case of the Indictment against Mr.

It was intimated on the part of the Clerk and the Officer that the instructions of last Meeting had been complied with. Mr.   appeared in his place as a Member of Court. The Presbytery took into consideration the proposed form of Indictment against Mr.

It was moved and seconded that this form be found relevant as an Indictment.

It was also moved and seconded that it be found irrelevant.

The votes having been marked, etc., etc.

The Presbytery accordingly resolve to serve the Indictment upon Mr.   as one which they have already found to be relevant. From which judgment Mr.   dissented, and protested for leave to complain to the Synod, promising, etc., etc.

The Presbytery ordered the Indictment to be now served in due form, notwithstanding the dissent and complaint, and find that Mr.   now ceases, *ipso facto*, to exercise the functions of his office.

d. *Probation of Indictment resolved on.*

Further, the Presbytery resolved to proceed to a proof of the Charges set forth in the aforesaid Indictment, in due form, according to the rules of the Church, at a Meeting to be held on the   day of   , at   o'clock; and they cited the Rev. A. B., *apud acta*, to attend said Meeting.

e. *Procedure sisted.*

The Presbytery finding that the Indictment, as an Indictment found to be relevant, has been served in due form upon Mr.   , but that a dissent and protest for leave to complain have been duly recorded and acted on, hereby sist all further procedure in the case until a final decision on the relevancy shall have been pronounced by the Synod.

The Minutes relative to Probation and other Procedure, until the issue of the Indictment, may be in terms corresponding to the nature of the case similar to those used in case of an Indictment prosecuted by Members of a Congregation, or by others duly qualified to act as prosecutors.

f. Decisions come to.

If signs of penitence have been given, and the offence proved does not demand so severe a punishment as deposition, but still that so much guilt has been proved as that some punishment is called for, the court may *suspend* the accused from the exercise of his Ministerial functions, and that either for a specified or unspecified period, as to the Presbytery may seem most proper in the circumstances of the case, and may declare the pastoral tie to be dissolved.

If the person accused be a Preacher of the Gospel, he is, in the event of the Indictment being proved, deprived of his licence, in which case the Minute may be in the following terms, namely :—The Presbytery therefore did, and hereby do, deprive the said Mr.   of his licence as a Preacher of the Gospel, declare that he cannot be admitted into any pulpit within the bounds of the Presbyterian Church of England, and that he is disqualified to accept a Call, or be received into any pastoral charge.

FORMS OF CITATIONS IN CASES OF DISCIPLINE.

In case of Parties present, in any of the Church Courts, Citation *apud acta* is valid.

When parties are not present written forms of Citation are necessary, and evidence that they have been duly served.

a. Citation of a Party in a Case.

1. To [*naming the person*]. Take notice that you are hereby cited to appear before the Session of   Church, in   , on the   day of   at   o'clock, to answer to the information against you for the sin or scandal of   laid to your charge.

(Signed)   , *Session Clerk*.
Served this   day of   , 18   .
          , *Church Officer*.

2. To the Rev. C. D., Minister of   Church, in

Take notice that you are hereby cited to appear before the Presbytery of   , within   at   , on the   day of   , at   o'clock, to answer to the Indictment, a copy of which is prefixed.

     (Signed) *Presbytery Clerk.*
Served this day of   , by
           , *Officer.*

b. *Citation of a Witness in a Case.*

To [*naming the person*]. Take notice that you are hereby cited to appear before the Session of   Church [*or*, before the Presbytery of   ] in   , on the   day of   , at   o'clock, to give evidence in the charge against   , now pending before said Session [*or*, Presbytery].

     (Signed) , *Clerk.*
Served this day of   , by
           , *Officer.*

FORMS OF INDICTMENT.

1.—IN CASE OF IMMORALITY.

Mr.   , Minister of the Church of   , in the Presbytery of   , you are indicted and accused at the instance of   , Moderator, and   and   , Members of the said Presbytery of   , [or if the Indictment is raised at the instance of the Members of the Congregation of   ], that albeit, by the Word of God, and the laws and discipline of the Presbyterian Church of England (here state the denomination of offence), is an offence of an heinous nature, unbecoming the character and the sacred profession of a Minister of the Gospel, and severely punishable by the laws and rules of the Church: yet true it is and of verity, that you, the said   , are guilty of the said offence in so far as, on the   twenty-first day of (*April*), eighteen hundred and eighty   ,[*] or on one or other of the days of that month, or of (*March*) immediately preceding, or of (*May*) immediately following, you, the said   , did, within the house in the town of   , then and now or lately occupied by   (here describe the circumstances of the offence), all which or part thereof, being found proven against you, the said   , by the said Presbytery of   , before which you are to be tried, in terms of your own public

---

[*] It is convenient to print the date thus.

confession, or after competent proof, you, the said   , ought to be punished according to the rules and discipline of the Church, and the usage observed in such cases, for the glory of God, the edification of the Church, and to the warning of others holding the same sacred office, not to commit the like offences in all time coming.

Signed at   , in name, presence, and by appointment of the Presbytery of   , this   day of   , 18   years, by

, *Moderator.*
, *Clerk.*

2.—In Case of Heresy.

Mr.   , Minister of the   Congregation at   , in the Presbytery of   , you are indicted and accused, at the instance of the said Presbytery of   , in connection with the Presbyterian Church of England,—That whereas the publishing and promulgating false and unsound doctrines, at variance with the Holy Scriptures and with the doctrines and Confession of Faith of the Presbyterian Church of England, by a Minister of the said Church, is an offence of an heinous nature and severely punishable; and more particularly, (1) Albeit the doctrine that moral evil has no real existence, but is such only in appearance and in reference to man's limited views; (2) As also the doctrine that native good and native tendencies to good, exist in a greater degree than evil and tendencies thereto, in the present estate and moral nature of man; (3) As also the doctrines, etc. . . . (13.) As also the denial of the doctrine that the Lord Jesus Christ is very God as well as very man, that He freely gave Himself a voluntary sacrifice unto death for sin, and that by His death He made a proper and real satisfaction to His Father in behalf of His people, are contrary to the Holy Scripture, and to the doctrine held by the Presbyterian Church of England, and the Confession of Faith, more especially to what is contained therein concerning (1, 2, 3, 4, 5, 8, 9) human depravity, the fall, and man's natural relation to God, (10, 11) grace and regeneration, (6) the ultimate condition of the impenitent, (7) justification of faith, (2) the authority and obligation of revelation and the Divine Law; and (13) the person and work of Christ; yet true it is and of verity, that you, the said Mr.   , hold and have promulgated the aforesaid tenets, and have avowed, published, and disseminated the same, in all or some of the books under-mentioned written by you, and published to the world,* namely :—

---

* When the Indictment is founded upon one or more sermons preached but not published, evidence of notes taken at the time by Members of the Church hearing the same may be referred to in the Indictment.

1. A Book entitled [*here copy title-page*].
2. A Book entitled, &c.; all which books were printed and published by you, Mr.   , or by others acting under your authority and instructions, in or about the years respectively mentioned in their respective title-pages; and which books, being to be used in evidence against you, are lodged in the hands of the Clerk to the Presbytery, that you may have an opportunity of seeing the same. Of all which books you have judicially acknowledged yourself to be the author, to the said Presbytery of   , by letter under your hand, dated   ; which books contain throughout an avowal, declaration, enforcement, and promulgation of the above-mentioned noxious, false, and unsound doctrines. More particularly, and without prejudice to the said generality—

1st. You, the said Mr.   , in the aforesaid work entitled, etc., and at pages   and   of the   volume of that work, made use of the following expressions, namely:—[*Here take in extract*].

2nd, etc.—And the aforesaid letter by you, acknowledging the authorship of the several books before written, as also the other letters under-mentioned, also written by you; as also the following Extracts from the Records of the said Presbytery of   ; as also the other papers and documents in the case under-mentioned, being to be used against you, are lodged with the Clerk of the Presbytery, or the person acting for him *pro tempore*, that you may have an opportunity of seeing the same:—[*Here follows list*].

All which, etc.

FORM OF DEPOSITION.

Form of Deposition used by Moderator of Presbytery or Synod.

In the name of the Lord Jesus Christ, the sole King and Head of this Church, and by virtue of the power and authority committed by Him to it, I do now solemnly depose you,   , Minister of   Church, in this Presbytery, from the office of the Holy Ministry, prohibiting and discharging you from exercising the same, or any part thereof, in all time coming, under the pain of the severest censure of the Church; and I do declare the pastoral charge of   Church, in this Presbytery, vacant, from and after the day and date of this sentence.

R.—MODEL TRUST DEED OF THE PRESBYTERIAN CHURCH OF ENGLAND.

EXTRACT MINUTE OF SYNOD HELD AT LONDON ON THE 25TH APRIL, 1879.

Inter alia, the Report of the Law and Historical Documents Committee was laid on the table by Dr. Leone Levi, Convener.

Resolved—The Synod receive the Report; approve and adopt the Draft Trust Deed now submitted; authorise the Committee to issue the Model Trust Deed as revised by Counsel, and to place the same in the hands of the Publications Committee for publication in a separate form for the use of the Church.

WILLIAM GRAHAM, D.D., Moderator.
WILLIAM M'CAW, Synod Clerk.

PREFACE.

The preparation of the Model Trust Deed was entrusted by the Synod in 1877 to the Law and Historical Documents Committee, in conjunction with the Church Building Committee. The terms were agreed to at a Conference held in March, 1878, between the two Committees, and the Deed was prepared by Counsel, by direction of the Law and Historical Documents Committee, and submitted to the Synod in the same year. The Synod referred the Model Trust Deed to the Presbyteries, and upon the reception of the returns from the Presbyteries, the Law and Historical Documents Committee revised the same, and re-submitted it to Counsel. The Deed thus carefully prepared was presented to the Synod in April, 1879, and the Synod approved and adopted the same.

The annexed is, therefore, the SYNOD'S MODEL TRUST DEED, to be used in all cases where a new Trust Deed is required.

The Deed being a Model, may not be adapted in all its details to cases where there is any speciality of tenure or otherwise. Different forms are appended for cases where the property is leasehold, and where the Trustees acquire further property for manse or school, whether freehold or leasehold. Whatever the speciality, however, care should be taken to insert in any Trust Deed the principal conditions of the Model Trust Deed, as regards the connection of the property with the Presbyterian Church of England, and adherence to the Standard Formulæ as specified in Clause III. of the Deed. The Agreement relative to the manse should be used where a dwelling-house is built or purchased for, or the use of the same is granted to, the Minister in office for the time being.

The Model Trust Deed does not describe the form of Church Government, or the several Judicatories of the Presbyterian Church, but refers in all cases to the Rules, Regulations, and Forms of Procedure, which may be approved and adopted from time to time by the Synod of the said Church. At this moment the Law and Historical Documents Committee are engaged in preparing the rules and forms of procedure in Church Courts, and when completed and recommended by the Synod for general use, these will constitute the common law, or common practice, of the Presbyterian Church of England.

New Trustees, whenever necessary, must be appointed at a general meeting of the congregation, in accordance with the mode indicated in the 13 & 14 Vict., c. xxviii., herein appended.

LEONE LEVI, *Convener.*

July, 1879

MODEL TRUST DEED.

[*These recitals to be used only when the Trustees are seized in fee of the property being of a freehold tenure. If the property is leasehold, substitute for the word "heir" the words "executors and administrators," and for the word "seized" substitute the word "possessed."*]

The Trustees in whom certain property is vested declaring the trusts of it in favour of the Presbyterian Church of England.

The parcels in respect of which the trusts are declared by this present instrument.

Witness.

To all to whom THESE PRESENTS SHALL COME SEND GREETING. WHEREAS the said   are seized of or entitled to with the appurtenances for an estate of inheritance in fee simple in possession free from incumbrances. AND WHEREAS the said   are desirous to stand and be seized of the said hereditaments and premises upon and for the trusts intents and purposes and in the manner hereinafter expressed.

NOW THESE PRESENTS WITNESS that for effectuating the said desire and in consideration of the premises IT IS HEREBY DECLARED AND AGREED that the said   their [heirs] and assigns shall stand and be [seized] of the said hereditaments and premises upon the trusts and with and subject to the powers provisos agreements and declarations hereinafter declared and contained concerning the same (that is to say)

Trusts for erection of Church and conveniences.

1.—UPON TRUST that they the said   and the survivors or survivor and their or his assigns (who are hereinafter referred to as the Trustees) do and shall with and out of the moneys now or hereafter to be possessed by them for that purpose as soon as conveniently may be after the execution of these trusts erect and build upon the said land and hereditaments or upon some part thereof a Church or Building for public religious worship in connection with the Synod of the Presbyterian Church of England with or without Vestry Sessionroom Schoolroom or Schoolrooms Lecture Hall Minister's House Teacher's House or any of them respectively and with or without all such other buildings conveniences and appurtenances of whatsoever nature or description and in such manner as the persons lawfully exercising control over the temporal affairs of the Congregation hereinafter referred to as the Managers shall from time to time deem expedient or necessary and shall in the execution of the trusts aforesaid act under the direction of such Managers.

MODEL TRUST DEED.

2.—AND UPON TRUST from time to time and at all times hereafter to permit and suffer the said Church or Building and other trust premises to be used and occupied for a place of Religious Worship and for the other purposes herein contained concerning the same.   *For religious and other purposes.*

3.—AND IT IS HEREBY DECLARED that the doctrines to be preached or taught in the said Church or in any School or Schools for religious or for secular and religious instruction in connection therewith and the worship to be observed and conducted in the said Church and the government and discipline of the Congregation from time to time belonging to the said Church and the ministrations and duties of the Ministers Elders Deacons or Managers and Members thereof shall be such as are consistent with the Presbyterian form of Church Government and agreeable to the following Standards of the Assembly of Divines convened at Westminster in the year 1643 (that is to say) the Confession of Faith and the Larger and Shorter Catechisms such Standards being interpreted or explained in case of any doubt or difficulty by the Ecclesiastical Association or Body now designated and known as the Synod of the Presbyterian Church of England the said interpretation being confirmed by a majority of Presbyteries of the aforesaid Church and whether such Synod shall or shall not at any time or times hereafter associate or unite itself with or take into union any other body or associated bodies of Christians of any denomination whatever adhering to the aforesaid Standards (which Synod is hereinafter referred to as the Synod) and also such as shall be consistent with and agreeable to such additional directions or rules as to worship government or discipline (if any) as may from time to time be prescribed or ordained by the Synod. PROVIDED ALWAYS that in case of the adoption at any time hereafter by the Synod or General Assembly of the said Church of a Compendium or Abridgment of the said Standards or a Declaration of Faith in harmony with the doctrines of the same as the Standard of the said Church the same shall be held as equivalent to the aforesaid Standards. PROVIDED ALSO that every such interpretation or explanation and additional directions or rules Abridgment or Declaration shall be entered in some book or document belonging to the Synod and signed by the Moderator and Clerk thereof.   *Doctrines and discipline to be taught and observed.*

4.—AND IT IS HEREBY DECLARED that the Congregation consisting of Ministers Elders Deacons or Managers and Members shall be subject to the Judicatories of the Presbyterian Church of England and that the administration of the affairs of the Congregation in all respects shall be in accordance with and regulated by   *The Congregation to be subject to the Judicatories of the Presbyterian Church of England, etc.*

the Presbyterian form of Church Government as interpreted explained and carried out by the rules regulations and forms of procedure as are or may be approved and adopted from time to time by the Synod of the said Church.

Powers of Session.

5.—AND IT IS HEREBY DECLARED that subject to the revision of the Presbytery hereinafter mentioned and of the Synod the superintendence and control of the spiritual and ecclesiastical affairs of the said Congregation shall be vested in the Session that is to say the Minister or Ministers and Elders thereof for the time being.

Deposition to take away all rights and powers in Minister or others deposed.

6.—AND IT IS HEREBY DECLARED that whenever any Minister Elder Deacon or Manager or other person shall be deposed suspended or removed from his office or shall cease to be such he shall *ipso facto* immediately cease to occupy any part of the said hereditaments and premises and to have any trust estate or interest in the said premises or exercise any function or office in the said Congregation and shall be absolutely deprived of all the civil and pecuniary rights emoluments stipend or salary to which by virtue of his office he would but for such sentence have been entitled and shall forthwith deliver up to the Trustees all such parts of the said trust estate and premises and all such deeds books papers moneys and effects belonging or relating thereto as may then be in his occupation possession or power.

Alterations and repairs of church and buildings.

Power to borrow money.

7.—AND IT IS HEREBY DECLARED that it shall be lawful for the Trustees at the request of the Managers to take down alter enlarge repair or rebuild the said church or other buildings and premises or any of them or any part or parts thereof. AND IT IS HEREBY FURTHER DECLARED that for the purposes of erecting and building the said Church Vestry Sessionroom Schoolroom or Schoolrooms Lecture Hall Minister's House Teacher's House and other conveniences and appurtenances hereinbefore mentioned or any of them or for the purpose of making such alterations enlargements reparations or rebuildings as aforesaid or any of them the Trustees may whenever they shall be requested so to do by the Managers with the consent in writing of the Presbytery to be signified under the hands of the Moderator and Clerk for the time being of the Presbytery raise borrow take up and receive whenever and as often as the Trustees or the major part of them see fit from any person or persons who shall be willing to advance and lend the same any sum or sums of money upon mortgage or lien of the said trust premises and for that purpose from time to time to convey and assure in fee or for any term or terms of years and with or without power of sale the said trust premises or

MODEL TRUST DEED. 155

any part thereof to any person or persons or to deposit the title-deeds of the said trust premises or any of them or to create any equitable charge or lien on the said trust premises or any of them for securing such sum or sums of money as may be necessary for the purposes aforesaid or any of them. PROVIDED ALWAYS that no Trustees or Trustee shall be bound to incur any personal responsibility for any debt or debts which may be contracted for any of the purposes aforesaid.

8.—AND IT IS HEREBY DECLARED that it shall be lawful for the Trustees at the request of the Managers with the consent of the Presbytery to be signified in writing under the hands of the Moderator and Clerk for the time being of the Presbytery at any time or times hereafter absolutely to sell and dispose of any such part or parts of the said hereditaments and premises either altogether or in parcels and for such price or prices as they may be able to obtain and to assure the same to the purchaser or purchasers freed and absolutely discharged from the trusts of these presents and the Trustees shall apply the money which shall arise from every such sale in discharging all the incumbrances liabilities and responsibilities whether personal or otherwise lawfully contracted or occasioned in execution of the trusts of these presents and subsequent thereto the surplus (if any) shall be paid to the Managers to be by them applied in such manner with the consent of the Presbytery to be signified in writing in manner aforesaid as they shall deem expedient on behalf of the Church. *Powers of disposition with consent of Presbytery. Proceeds of sale, how to be applied.*

9.—AND IT IS HEREBY DECLARED that if in the discretion of the Managers it shall at any time or times hereafter be deemed necessary or expedient to procure another place of worship or other building or buildings for the use of the Congregation then and in every such case it shall be lawful for the Trustees with the consent of the Presbytery to be signified in writing as aforesaid to sell the said trust premises or any part thereof either altogether or in parcels and for such price or prices as they may be able to obtain and to assure the same to the purchaser or purchasers freed and absolutely discharged from the trusts of these presents. And the money arising from such last-mentioned sale or sales shall in the first place be applied in discharging all such incumbrances liabilities and responsibilities as aforesaid and subject thereto the surplus (if any) shall be applied by the Trustees in or towards the procuring or completing of such other place of worship or buildings and conveniences (if any) as may have been contemplated on making such sale. And the residue (if any) shall be paid to the Managers to be by them applied in such manner and for such purposes as hereinafter in the 10th Clause mentioned. *Powers of disposition of unoccupied place of worship when a more suitable site is obtained.*

Powers to let.	10.—AND IT IS HEREBY DECLARED that if at any time hereafter the pew-rents voluntary contributions of the Members of the Congregation or other available sources of income in connection with or belonging to the said trust estate and premises shall be inadequate to discharge the interest of any money borrowed and to maintain the preaching of the Gospel and the administration of Ordinances in or upon the said trust premises it shall be lawful for the Trustees on specifying the object and obtaining the consent of the Presbytery signified in writing as aforesaid from time to time or at any time to let the said trust premises or any part or parts thereof for any term of years not exceeding seven years altogether for such rent fine or other sum of money as they may be able to obtain and after discharging all expenses and liabilities incident to the execution of the trusts of these presents to invest or pay over the surplus in such manner as shall be approved of by the Presbytery to be signified in writing as aforesaid in order that the same may accumulate until the Presbytery shall consider it expedient to resume the preaching of the Gospel and the administration of Ordinances in or upon the said trust premises.
Power of disposition without consent of Presbytery.	But if the Trustees shall be unable to let the said trust premises in manner aforesaid for so much money as will suffice to defray the current charges for interest of debt (if any) and for repairs insurance and other necessary expenses and if they shall desire to retire and be discharged from the execution of the said trust (no proper persons being found to undertake the execution of the said trusts) then and in every such case it shall be lawful for the Trustees without any such consent of the Presbytery as aforesaid to sell and dispose of the said trust premises or any part thereof either altogether or in parcels and for such price or prices as they may be able to obtain and to assure or cause to be assured the same to the purchaser or purchasers freed and absolutely discharged from the trusts of these presents.
Proceeds of disposition under last-mentioned powers.	And the money arising from such last-mentioned sale or sales shall in the first place be applied in discharging all such incumbrances liabilities and responsibilities as aforesaid and subject thereto the surplus (if any) shall be paid to the Treasurer for the time being of the Synod to be applied under the direction and at the discretion of the Synod for the
No sale however under such last-mentioned power to take place unless previous intimation be given to the Presbytery and Synod.	spiritual benefit of the Congregation or for such other religious purposes in connection with the Synod as to the Synod shall seem meet. PROVIDED ALWAYS AND IT IS HEREBY DECLARED that no sale shall be made under the power contained in this clause unless the Trustees or the major part of them shall have given notice in writing to the Moderator and Clerk of the Presbytery three calendar months at least prior to the annual meeting of the Synod and to the Moderator and Clerk of the Synod

of the intention to make such sale and of the reason for the same nor unless the Presbytery and the Synod shall from the time of the giving of the first of such notices down to the expiration of three calendar months next after such annual meeting respectively refuse or neglect to give or provide the Trustees with such pecuniary assistance as would enable them to continue the execution of the trusts of these presents or refuse or neglect to provide other Trustees to take upon themselves the execution thereof. AND IT IS HEREBY DECLARED that at any time after the receipt of any such notice as aforesaid it shall be lawful for the Presbytery or for the Synod to appoint such persons to be Trustees of the said hereditaments and premises as they or either of them may think proper. *If notice of sale be given by Trustees because of their inability to find fresh Trustees, the Presbytery may appoint Trustees.*

11.—AND IT IS HEREBY DECLARED that it shall not be incumbent on any mortgagee lessee or purchaser to inquire into the necessity or propriety of any mortgage demise or sale or the purposes for or the circumstances under which the same may be made nor whether any Minister Elder Deacon or Manager has been duly appointed or whether any such consent as aforesaid from the Presbytery or the Synod or either of them has been given and signed or at all previously obtained nor to inquire whether any notice or notices was or were given to the Presbytery or the Synod or either of them or any other person or persons or was or were valid nor whether the Presbytery or the Synod or either of them refused pecuniary assistance or to appoint other Trustee as aforesaid nor whether the Managers had deemed it necessary or expedient to procure another place of worship or other buildings as aforesaid nor otherwise into the propriety or validity of such mortgage demise or sale nor be affected by express notice that all or any of the foregoing requisites or directions for a mortgage demise or sale or any other antecedent steps or directions to the due execution of any of the trusts or powers herein contained have not been complied with. *Protection to mortgagees, lessees, and purchasers.*

12.—AND IT IS HEREBY DECLARED that the receipt and receipts of a majority of the Trustees shall in all cases of payment made to them or any of them as such Trustees or Trustee as aforesaid be a full discharge to the person or persons entitled to such receipt or receipts his her or their heirs executors administrators and assigns for all mortgage moneys purchase moneys rents or other moneys therein respectively expressed and acknowledged to have been received by any such Trustees or Trustee as aforesaid. AND it shall not be incumbent upon any such mortgagee or mortgagees lessee or lessees purchaser or purchasers or any of them or any other person or persons his her or their executors administrators or assigns paying *Receipts of Trustees good discharge. Further protection to mortgagees, lessees, and purchasers.*

money to such Trustees to see to the application or be answerable or accountable for the loss mis-application or non-application of such purchase or other money or any part thereof for which a receipt or receipts shall be so respectively given as aforesaid.

Indemnity to Trustees.

13.—AND IT IS HEREBY DECLARED that the Trustees shall not nor shall any of them their or any of their heirs executors or administrators or any of them be chargeable or accountable for any involuntary loss suffered by them or any of them nor any one or more of them for any other or others of them nor for more money than shall come to their respective hands nor for injury done by others to the said trust premises or to any part or parts thereof.

Minister, Elder, or Trustee when elected to become a Trustee within the meaning of the 13 & 14 Vict. c. 28, unless he declines the Trusteeship. Cessation of Trusteeship.

14.—AND IT IS HEREBY DECLARED that any person who shall be elected as Minister Elder Deacon or Manager of the Congregation or of the Presbyterian Church shall immediately thereupon be eligible to become a Trustee within the intent and meaning of the Act 13 and 14 Vict. cap. 28 and being so elected unless he declines the trusteeship he shall continue such Trustee during the time he shall be Minister Elder Deacon or Manager jointly with the other Trustees if any or solely as the case may be except as hereinafter in this clause provided. If any Minister Elder Deacon Manager or Trustee for the time being shall voluntarily withdraw from or shall be excluded from membership therein by any sentence as herein provided or cease to be a Minister or Communicant or Seatholder in the Congregation or of or in some other Congregation of the Synod such Trustee shall thereupon cease to be a Trustee of these presents in the same manner as if he were actually dead.

Directions for the appointment of fresh Trustees.

15.—AND IT IS HEREBY FURTHER DECLARED that whenever the number of Trustees acting under or in pursuance of these presents and whether the legal estate in the said premises shall be vested in them or not shall be diminished or if at any time it shall be deemed advisable to increase the number of Trustees it shall be lawful and if the number be reduced below four it shall be imperative for the Congregation to appoint so many fit and proper persons under the Act 13 and 14 Vict. cap. 28 as they may deem expedient to be Trustees of the said piece or parcel of land Church hereditaments and premises. AND IT IS HEREBY DECLARED that in order to save the expenses of frequent conveyances every Trustee so appointed shall be fully competent to act immediately upon his election or appointment although the legal estate in the said trust premises may not by the said act or otherwise be effectually vested in him nor shall it be incumbent on any lessee mortgagee or purchaser to call for or insist on such conveyance being obtained but whenever the number of Trustees in whom the legal estate is vested for the time being shall be reduced below four the said trust estate and premises shall without delay be duly conveyed to and vested in the continuing and new Trustees or to or in the new Trustees solely as the case may be upon the trusts herein contained or referred to or such of them as may be subsisting and capable of taking effect.

Peremptory direction for appointment of fresh Trustees whenever reduced below four.

16.—AND IT IS HEREBY DECLARED that notwithstanding anything herein contained to the contrary it shall be lawful for the Congregation by a majority of votes at a meeting duly convened and the sanction of the Session Presbytery and Synod such last-mentioned sanction to be signified under the hands of the Moderator and Clerk for the time being of the Synod and to be written in or upon the deed or instrument in writing in or by which any new or amended trusts may be declared to alter revoke or annul or to add to or diminish amend explain or modify all or any of the trusts powers provisoes agreements and declarations herein contained and to declare such new and additional or other trusts powers provisoes agreements and declarations as the Synod may permit without reference or regard to the original trusts powers provisoes declarations and agreements herein expressed or contained or referred to or the usage or practice of the Congregation or their government discipline mode of worship or any other matter or thing whatsoever and without being controlled or restrained by any such trusts usage or practice so nevertheless that such alterations revocations and additional or diminished amended explained or modified trusts powers provisoes or declarations shall not interfere with restrain or affect that portion and that portion only of the trusts hereinbefore in the third clause contained which directs that the doctrines to be preached and taught in the said Church or in any School or Schools in connection therewith and the worship to be observed and conducted in the said Church and the government and discipline of the Congregation from time to time belonging to the said Church and the ministration and duties of the Minister or Ministers Elders Deacons Managers and Members thereof shall be such as are consistent with the Presbyterian form of Church government and agreeable to the aforesaid Westminster Standards so explained or interpreted as hereinbefore mentioned and such altered revoked and new or additional or other trusts powers provisoes and declarations in like manner as these presents shall from time to time and at all times be and remain subject to this present clause and to the power therein contained.

General power of revocation but not to affect fundamental part of the 3rd Clause.

In the event of General Assembly being formed all the powers vested by the deed in the Synod shall be held vested in the said General Assembly.

17.—AND IT IS HEREBY DECLARED that in case the Synod shall determine to institute or form part of a General Assembly solely or in conjunction with any other Church or Chuches adhering to the Standards hereinbefore mentioned then every sentence and decision of the Synod shall be subject to the revision and control of such General Assembly and the powers and authorities hereinbefore in the 3rd Clause contained shall thenceforth be vested in and exercised by such General Assembly and not by the Synod and it shall also be lawful for such General Assembly to exercise any other or others of the powers herein mentioned as belonging to the Synod and for that purpose such General Assembly shall have original powers and jurisdiction concurrent with the powers and jurisdiction of the Synod and the powers and stipulations hereinbefore contained which have reference to the Synod and the Moderator and Clerk thereof shall henceforth apply to and be exercised by such General Assembly and the Moderator and Clerk or other similar officers thereof and the powers and stipulations herein contained which have reference to the Presbyteries composing or forming part of the Synod and to the Churches which have reference to the Synod and the Moderator and Clerk thereof and Congregations within the bounds or forming part of such Presbyteries and to members of such Churches or Congregations shall henceforth apply to and be exercised by the Presbyteries composing or forming part of such General Assembly and the Churches and Congregations within the bounds and forming part of such last-mentioned Presbyteries and the members of such last-mentioned Churches and Congregations.

18.—AND IT IS HEREBY LASTLY DECLARED that if such General Assembly shall resolve or declare that the Synod has ceased to exist or that the same shall cease to exist at any future time to be appointed by such General Assembly and if such General Assembly shall form the Presbyteries of which it shall or may be composed into two or more Provincial Synods subordinate to such General Assembly then the powers and stipulations hereinbefore contained shall thenceforth apply to and be exercised by the Provincial Synod within the bounds of which the said trust premises shall be situate or of which the said Congregation shall form a part and the Moderator and Clerk or other similar officers of such Provincial Synod. PROVIDED ALWAYS that it shall be lawful to appeal from such Provincial Synod to the said General Assembly or Association whose decision shall be final.

IN WITNESS &c

APPENDIX A.

To be added in the Recitals in the Model Form.

1. [WHEN THE PROPERTY IS LEASEHOLD.]
WHEREAS the said
are entitled to
      with the appurtenances for the residue of the term of years commencing from the
 day of   18 subject to the rents and covenants contained in the Indenture of Lease of the
 day of   AND WHEREAS the said
are desirous to stand possessed of the said hereditaments and premises upon and for the trusts intents and purposes and in the manner hereinafter expressed.

2. [WHEN THE PROPERTY IS COPYHOLD.]
WHEREAS the said   are seized
of or entitled to   being Copyhold of
the Manor of   in the County of
  with the appurtenances for an Estate of inheritance in possession to them and to their heirs according to the custom of the said Manor.
AND WHEREAS the said   are desirous to stand and be seized of the said hereditaments and premises upon and for the trusts intents and purposes and in the manner hereinafter expressed.

APPENDIX B.

In the event of the Trustees purchasing further property for Manse or Schools the following conveyance to be used if Freehold.

This Indenture made the   day of
18 BETWEEN   of the one part and
  of the other part WHEREAS the said
  has agreed with the said
 and   for the absolute sale to them of the hereditaments hereinafter described and the inheritance thereof in fee simple in possession free from incumbrances at the price of £ and the said
  have requested that the said hereditaments may be conveyed to them upon the trusts intents and purposes and in manner hereinafter declared NOW THIS INDENTURE WITNESSETH that in pursuance of the said Agreement and in consideration of the sum of £

upon the execution of these presents paid by the said
          to the said   (the receipt
whereof the said   doth hereby acknowledge
and from the same doth hereby release the said
) the said   doth by this deed which
is intended to be enrolled in the Chancery Division of the
High Court of Justice grant unto the said
and their heirs ALL   TO HAVE AND
TO HOLD the hereditaments and premises hereby granted
or expressed so to be unto and to the use of the said
               and   their
heirs and assigns for ever. But upon such and the same
Trusts and to and for such and the same intents and purposes and with under and subject to such and the same
powers provisions declarations and agreements as are expressed declared or referred to in a certain Deed poll
dated the   day of   18   and
under the hands and seals of   and which
Deed poll is enrolled in the Chancery Division of the High
Court of Justice and is an instrument in writing for the
settlement of a plot of ground Church and other buildings
situate at   for Religious Worship and
other purposes therein mentioned on behalf of a body of
Christian Members of the Presbyterian Church of England.

APPENDIX C.

In the event of the Trustees purchasing further property for Manse or Schools the following conveyance to be used if Leasehold.

This Indenture made the   day of
18 BETWEEN   of the one part
and   of the other part WHEREAS by an
Indenture of Lease dated the   day of
           and made between   of the one part
and the said   of the other part ALL

that were demised by the said   unto the said
          the executors administrators and assigns
from the   day of   then last for the term of
    years at the yearly rent of £   and subject to
the covenants and conditions in the said Indentures of
Lease contained and on the part of the Lessee his executors administrators and assigns to be observed and performed AND WHEREAS the said   hath
agreed with the said   and
for the sale to them of the hereditaments and premises
comprised in the said Indenture of Lease for the residue
now unexpired for the said term of   years for

the sum of £   and the said   and
have requested that the said hereditaments and premises may be assigned to them upon the trusts intents and purposes and in the manner hereinafter declared NOW THIS INDENTURE WITNESSETH that in pursuance of the said Agreement and in consideration of the sum of £   paid by the said   and
to the said   (the receipt whereof the said   doth hereby acknowledge and from the same doth hereby release the said
and   ) The said   doth by this Deed which is intended to be enrolled in the Chancery Division of the High Court of Justice assign unto the said   and   their executors administrators and assigns the hereditaments and premises comprised in and demised by the hereinafter recited Indenture or expressed so to be And all the estate right title interest claim and demand whatsoever of the said   in to and upon the said premises and every part thereof TO HAVE AND TO HOLD the hereditaments and premises hereby assigned or expressed so to be unto the said   and   their executors administrators and assigns for all the residue now unexpired of the said term of   years subject to the rent reserved by the said Indenture of Lease and the covenants and conditions in the same Indenture contained and which henceforth on the part of the Lessee his executors administrators or assigns ought to be observed and performed But upon such and the same trusts and to and for such and the same intents and purposes and with under and subject to such and the same provisions declarations and agreements as are expressed declared or referred to in a certain Deed poll dated the   day of   18   and under the hands and seals of   and which Deed poll is enrolled in the Chancery Division of the High Court of Justice and in an instrument for the settlement of a plot of ground Church and other hereditaments situate at   for Religious Worship and other purposes therein mentioned on behalf of a body of Christian Members of the Presbyterian Church of England AND IT IS HEREBY DECLARED that every power provision trust clause matter and thing in the same Deed poll contained concerning the freehold hereditaments thereby granted shall be applicable and effectual to all intents and purposes as if they had been herein repeated and set forth at length with such variations if any as the difference in the nature of the title and tenure of the hereditaments and premises thereby and hereby assured requires.

APPENDIX D.

13 & 14 Vict., Cap. xxviii.

AN ACT to render more simple and effectual the titles by which Congregations or Societies for purpose of Religious Worship or Education in England and Ireland hold property for such purposes.

[15th July, 1850.]

Property conveyed for religious or educational purposes to vest in successors without conveyance.

WHEREAS it is expedient to render more simple and effectual the titles by which Congregations or Societies associated together for the purpose of maintaining Religious Worship or promoting Education in England, Wales, or Ireland may hold the property required for such purposes: Be it therefore enacted by the Queen's Most Excellent Majesty, by and with the advice and consent of the Lords Spiritual and Temporal, and Commons, in this present Parliament assembled, and by the authority of the same. That wherever freehold, leasehold, copyhold, or customary Property in England or Wales has been or hereafter shall be acquired by any Congregation or Society or body of Persons associated for religious purposes or for the promotion of Education, as a Chapel, Meeting House, or other place of Religious Worship, or as a dwelling-house for the Ministers of such Congregation, with offices, garden, and glebe, or land in the nature of glebe, for his use, or as a schoolhouse, with Schoolmaster's house, garden and playground, or as a College, Academy, or Seminary, with or without grounds for air, exercise, or recreation, or as a hall or rooms for the meeting or transaction of the business of such Congregation or Society or body of persons, and wherever the conveyance, assignment, or other assurance of such property has been or may be taken to or in favour of a Trustee or Trustees to be from time to time appointed, or of any party or parties named in such conveyance, assignment, or other assurance, or subject to any trust for the Congregation or Society or body of persons, or of the individuals composing the same, such conveyance, assignment, or other assurance shall not only vest the freehold, leasehold, copyhold, or customary property thereby conveyed or otherwise assured in the party or parties named therein; but shall also effectually vest such freehold, leasehold, copyhold, or customary property in their successors in office for the time being, and the old continuing Trustees, if any, jointly, or if there be no old continuing Trustees, then in such successors for the time being wholly, chosen and appointed in the manner provided or referred to in or by such conveyance, assignment, or other assurance, or in any separate deed or instrument declaring the Trust thereof, or if no mode of appointment be therein set forth, prescribed, or referred to, or if the power of appointment be lapsed, then in such manner as shall be agreed upon by such Congregation or Society or body of persons, upon such and the like Trusts, and with, under, and subject to the same powers and provisions as are contained or referred to in such conveyance, assignment, or other assurance, or in any such separate deed or instrument, or upon which such property is held, and that without any transfer, assignment, conveyance, or other assurance whatsoever, anything in such conveyance, assignment, or other assurance, or in any such separate deed or instrument, contained to the contrary notwithstanding: Provided always, that in case of any appointment of a new Trustee or Trustees, or of the conveyance of the legal estate in any such property being made as heretofore was by law required, the same shall be as valid and effectual to all intents and purposes as if this Act had not passed.

II.—AND BE IT ENACTED: That where such property shall be of copyhold or customary tenure, and liable to the payment of any fine with or without a heriot, on the death or alienation of the Tenant thereof, it shall be lawful for the Lord or Lady of the Manor of which such property shall be holden, on the next appointment of a new Trustee or Trustees thereof, and at the expiration of every period of forty years thereafter, so long as such property shall belong to or be held in trust for such Congregation or Society or body of persons, or other party or parties to whom such property may have been or shall be conveyed for their benefit, to receive and take a sum corresponding to the fine and heriot, if any, which would have been payable by law upon the death or alienation of the tenant or tenants thereof; and such payments shall be in full of all fines payable to the Lord or Lady of the Manor of which such property is holden, while the same shall remain the property or be held in trust for such Congregation or Society or body of persons; and the Lord or Lady of such Manor shall have all such powers for the recovery of such sums as such Lord or Lady would have had in the event of the tenant or tenants of such property having died or having alienated the same. *Providing for payment in lieu of fines on death or alienation of property of copyhold or customary tenure.*

III.—AND BE IT ENACTED: That for the purpose of preserving evidence of every such choice and appointment of a new Trustee or new Trustees, and of the person and persons in whom such charitable estates and property shall so from time to time become legally vested, every such choice and appointment of a new Trustee or new Trustees shall be made to appear by some deed under the hand and seal of the Chairman for the time being of the meeting at which such choice and appointment shall be made, and shall be executed in the presence of such meeting, and attested by two or more credible witnesses, *Appointment of new trustees to be made appear by deed.*

which deed may be in the form or to the like effect of the Schedule to this Act annexed, or as near thereto as circumstances will allow, and may be given and shall be received as evidence in all courts and proceedings in the same manner and on the like proof as deeds under seal, and shall be evidence of the truth of the several matters and things therein contained.

Act extended to Ireland.

IV.—AND BE IT ENACTED: that the provisions of this Act shall extend to that part of the United Kingdom called Ireland.

Act may be amended, etc.

V.—AND BE IT ENACTED: That this Act may be amended or repealed by any Act to be passed in the present Session of Parliament, except so far as the contrary shall be made to appear.

SCHEDULE TO WHICH THIS ACT REFERS.

MEMORANDUM of the Church and Appointment of new Trustees of the [*describe the Chapel, School, or other buildings and property*] situate   in the parish [*or Township*] of   in the County [*Riding, Division, City, or Place*] of   at a meeting duly convened and held for that purpose in the [*Vestry of the said Chapel*] on the [*25th day of April*, 1880.]

A.B. of

Chairman,

Names and description of all the Trustees on the constitution or last appointment of Trustees made the day of

> A. B.
> C. D.
> E. F.
> G. H.

Names and description of all the Trustees in whom the said (Chapel) and premises now becomes legally vested.

First. I. K. ⎫
L. M. ⎬ *Old Continuing Trustees.*
N. O. ⎭

Second. P. Q. ⎫
R. S. ⎬ *New Trustees now chosen and appointed.*
T. U. ⎭

Dated this   day of

W. H.   (L. S.)
Chairman of the said Meeting.

Signed, sealed, and delivered by the said W. H. as Chairman of the said Meeting, at   and in the presence of the said Meeting, on the day and year aforesaid in the presence of   V. X.
                    Y. Z.

The blanks and parts in italic to be filled up as the case may be.

INDEX.

A

	PAGE
Absence of a Member of Court	2
Adherents in a Congregation	5, 33, 108
Admission of Members of a Congregation	5, 12, 119
,, Ministers, Congregations, Probationers, and Students from other Churches	37, 38, 43, 44, 111, 117
Admonition	63
Affirmation by a Witness	118
Aid to Accused	65

Appeals:
From Deacons' Court or Board of Managers	18
From one Church Court to another	37, 44
Procedure in	5, 51, 52, 123, 138
To a Civil Tribunal	2

Arrears	7, 21
Articles of the Faith	1
Assessors to a Session	9
,, ,, Presbytery	23
Associates of Presbytery	23
Audit	15, 18, 22, 128
Auditors	16, 17, 109, 123

B

Baptism	5
Baptized Members, Roll of	13
Board of Managers	16
Buildings, Use of Church	18, 22
,, Sale of	29

C

Call to a Minister	6, 32, 33
,, Forms of	107, 108
,, Form of Concurrence in	108
,, Procedure at giving of	32–34, 131–134
,, Signatures to	33, 108
,, Procedure at disposal of, to a Minister in a Pastoral Charge	35, 36, 134, 141
,, Commissioners in case of	36
Calvinistic Methodist Church of Wales, Relationship to the	4
Catechisms, Larger and Shorter	1
Censures, Church	63
,, ,, Removal of	64
Certificate, Right of Member to a	5, 13

Certificates, Forms of	112, 113
Church Building Fund	90–94
„ New	129
Citation in cases of Discipline	56, 57, 146, 147
Collections	13, 18, 44, 128
College, Theological	97–103
„ Senatus	97
„ Board of Examination	97
„ Course of Study	97, 98
„ Rules of Admission	98–100
„ „ Examinations	101
„ Fees	101
„ Residence	101
„ Scholarships	101, 102, 103
„ Exhibitions	102, 103
Commissions, Elders'	23, 24
„ Forms of	114
„ to Presbytery	114
„ to Synod	114
„ Sustaining of	23, 72
Commissioners to a Presbytery	6
Committees of Synod	44, 72
Communion Rolls	5, 8, 13, 27
„ „ Attesting of	13
„ „ Revising of	13, 27, 120
Complaints	44, 50, 51
„ Procedure in	51, 123, 139
Confession of Accused, Effect of	66
Congregation, Constitution of	5
„ Government of	5
„ Members of	5, 6
„ Adherents of	5
„ Ministerial Support in	6, 7
„ Formation of new	6
„ Meetings of	7, 18, 115, 116
„ Mission Stations of	8
„ Districts of	122, 127
„ Forms of Minutes of Meetings of	129, 130
„ Visitation of	139, 141
Contumacy	57, 64
Council, Federal	8
Counsel, Professional	65
Courts of the Church	2
„ „ Procedure in	47–53
„ „ Discipline by	65–69

D

Deacons, Election and Ordination of	13, 15, 110, 116, 124
Deacons' Court: Constitution	15
„ Official Members	15

		PAGE
Deacons' Court: President	. . . . . .	15
,, Meetings	. . . . .	16, 17
,, Functions and Duties	. . . .	17, 18
,, Forms of Minutes of	. . .	126–129
Debt, Power of contracting	. . . . . .	17, 22
Declarations, Forms of	. . . . . .	117, 118
Deposition	. . . .	64, 149
Deprivation of Licence	. . . . . .	64, 146
Diaconate, The	. . . .	19–22
Directory for Worship	. . . . . .	1
Discipline	. . . .	54–69
Dissent, Right of	. . . .	2, 49
,, Procedure in	. . . . .	49, 50, 123
,, Reasons for	. . . . . .	49, 50

E

Edicts, Forms of	109–111
Elders, Election of	9, 10, 116, 124
,, Ordination and Admission . .	10, 11, 118, 124, 125
,, Tenure of the Office of, in a Congregation .	11
,, Duties of	13
,, Representative, in Presbytery and Synod	14, 114
Evidence, Rules of	61, 62
Extracts of Minutes	12, 25

F

Fama	31, 68, 141
Federal Council of Three Churches . . .	3
Formulas	103
1. For use at Ordination of a Minister . .	103–105
2. ,, Licensing of Preachers . .	105, 106
3. ,, Ordination of Elders . .	106, 107
4. ,, ,, Deacons . .	107
Free Church of Scotland, Relationship to the . .	3
Funds:	
Aged and Infirm Ministers'	80
Sustentation	76
Home Mission	85–94
Widows' and Orphans'	81

G

Government of the Church	2

H

Heresy, Indictment for	148

		PAGE
Indictment		28, 58
,,	Forms of	147–149
,,	Right to call for	68
,,	Rules of	58
,,	Effect of Service of	67, 142
,,	Relevancy of	60, 142
,,	Probation of	143
,,	Procedure upon	58
,,	Decision upon	143, 144
Induction of Ministers		35, 36, 135, 136

J

Judicial Committee	28, 44
Jurisdiction	28, 29, 42, 66, 67, 68

L

Legal Adviser	28
Licence, Certificate of	31, 112
Licentiates	31, 34

M

Managers, Board of		16
,,	Qualifications of	16
,,	Election of	16, 116
,,	Retirement of	16
,,	Chairman of the Board of	16
,,	Official Members of the Board of	16
,,	Meetings of the Board of	16, 17
,,	Functions of the Board of	17
,,	Forms of Minutes of	126–129
Membership of the Church		1
Memorial or Petition		118
Memorials		53
Minister, Election of		13, 32, 33, 126, 129
,,	Responsibility of	12
Minutes, Forms of		119–149
Model Trust Deed		150–166
Moderator of Presbytery		24, 25
,,	Session	9
,,	Synod	39, 40
Motions, Order of putting		26, 33

N

Notice of Motions	26
Notices, Forms of	115, 116

O

Offence, Charge of	56
Order, Book of	vi.–viii.
„ Call to	42
„ of Business in Presbytery	26
Ordination of Ministers	34, 35, 117, 134, 135
„ Elders	118, 125
„ Deacons	118, 125
Overtures, Procedure in	28, 43, 47, 136

P

Papers, Distribution of, in Cases	53
„ for the Synod	41
Petition, Right of, and Transmission of	6
Petitions, Procedure in	13, 53, 138, 142
Praise, Service of	12, 17
Preachers, Licensing of	29, 30
Preaching Stations, Formation of	6, 140
Presbyterian Alliance	4
Presbyterian Church in Ireland, Relationship to the	3
Presbytery, The, Constitution and Officials of	23–25
„ „ Meetings of	25
„ „ Ordinary	25–27
„ „ Special	27
„ „ Order of Business at	26
„ „ Functions and Duties of	28, 29
„ „ Forms of Minutes of Meetings of	130–149
Probationers	31, 94
Probationers' Rolls	94, 95
„ Fees	96
Procedure common to all the Courts	47–53
Property of the Church	29, 129
„ „ Congregation	17

Q

Quorum, of Session	12
„ Deacons' Court	15
„ Board of Managers	16
„ Presbytery	25
„ Synod	40

R

Rebuke	63
Records	7, 12, 75
Reference	44
„ Procedure in	48, 49, 137, 138
Relation to other Churches	2–4
Relevancy of Indictment	60, 69

Relief of the Poor	17
Representatives of Sessions	14
Resignation of Ministers	31, 111
" Elders	13
" Deacons	13
Restoration of Offenders	65
Rights of Members	5, 6, 7, 8
" Speakers	42
Roll of baptized Members	13

S

Schemes of the Church	18, 21
Seat-letting	128
Session, Constitution of the	9
" Meetings	11
" Minutes	12, 27
" Functions and Duties	12, 13, 14
" Forms of Minutes of	119–126
" Representative of, in Presbytery	120
" " " Synod	120, 121
Standards of the Church	1
Standing Orders of the Synod	71–75
Stipend of Minister	7, 21
Students, Admission of	40
" Examination of	29, 31
" Transference of	30
Sunday Schools	13, 121
Supper, The Lord's	72, 119
Suspension	63, 64, 67, 146
Sustentation Fund Act	6, 76–80
Synod, Membership of	39
" Procedure of	40, 42
" Committees of	40–42
" Standing Orders of	71–75
" Functions and Duties of	42
" Legislative	42, 43
" Administrative	43, 44
" Judicial	44
" Commission of	46
" Corresponding Members of	2, 3, 4

T

Transference of Ministers	35, 36, 110, 133, 134
Treasurer of Deacons' Court	15
Trial, Summary	58
" on Indictment	58–61, 66, 142–146
Trials for Licence to Preach	29, 30
Trust Deeds of Congregations	16, 22
Trustees, Election of	7

U

United Presbyterian Church, Relation to the . . . PAGE 2

V

Vacancy in the Pastorate 31–33, 109, 115
Vote, Chairman's 15, 16
 „ Moderator's 2
Voting, Order of 26, 74, 75
 „ Right of, in Congregations 5, 7, 10

W

Week-day Schools. 28
Westminster Confession of Faith 1
Word of God 1
Worship, Public 12, 18, 28, 40

www.ingramcontent.com/pod-product-compliance
Lightning Source LLC
Chambersburg PA
CBHW031444160426
43195CB00010BB/845